LOOSE TALK

COLLECTED

Les Cowan

Published by

Information Plus,
3 Hill of Heddle
Finstown,
Orkney.
KW17 2LH

www.information-plus.co.uk

Printed by:

The Orcadian, Hell's Half Acre, Kirkwall

ISBN   978-0-9554644-1-6

Busted & Coldplay or Stevie Wonder & Pink Floyd?

Isn't that what the generation gap is for?

Among the laws of parenting (along with "Do as I say, not as I do" and "I would never have spoken like that to my father") is another golden rule, "Thou shalt not like the same music as your kids". Saying you like bands your kids think are cool can only have one of two effects. Either the kids in question will smell a rat, start asking you pop quiz questions you haven't a hope of answering (who is the lead singer of Busted and how many members are in Gorillaz), or in an effort to swot up you'll end up listening to this drivel so much you might actually get to like it. Both are of course equally ghastly outcomes.

For, of course, as we all know, like the void between Abraham and Lazarus, the generation gap is firmly fixed, unbridgeable and isn't likely to change any time soon. So even if Busted (sorry just to pick on you lads) were the T-Rex of the new millennium, guitar riffs drifting over the void become so distorted by turbulence and drifting clouds of prejudice that by the time they get to the parental bank they do in fact sound genuinely awful. So don't pretend that racket is harmonious and mellow and you really like it. It isn't and you don't. Admit it and do your kids, yourself and your musical integrity a favour.

And having discovering the principle, it's not long before you'll notice it applying to other things too. Ever since William Hague famously wore his baseball cap the wrong way round on a fairground ride, there has been a dawning awareness that you can never be too careful or conservative (small "c" please) about what you wear in public when the urge to look cool begins to bite. So sew up the holes in your jeans, forget about swear word anagrams on your tee-shirt and stick to chinos. I'm not advocating of course that you go to extremes and haul out the salmon pink heat sensitive trousers you thought looked groovy when you were 14 (ok – maybe it was just me) or the platforms you couldn't wear then, now or any time in between. Just act your age not your beanie hat size. Kids expect that. It reinforces their prejudices too and hence makes everyone a lot more comfortable.

And if all this sounds far too negative – the total lifestyle equivalent of "What not to Wear", let me make some positive suggestions. Hire a classic car for the weekend – something you couldn't afford at the time and have been dribbling over ever since. Give in to the urge – maybe you won't hate yourself in the morning after all. Watch the band touring dates and go and see some aging rockers you missed first, second and possibly third time round. Buy a turntable from the Past Times catalogue and see if Led Zep IV sounds just as loud and rebellious as when you were trying to revise for your O grades. Don't throw the Ramblers Magazine directly in the bin next time it drops on the mat. Maybe a walking holiday in the Dordogne is exactly what you need for mind, body and spirit, notwithstanding the slimming effect on your bank account as well. If you've always wanted to take up ballroom dancing or train spotting (ok – Scottish country dancing and bird watching in Orkney) do it. You're not going to sink any lower in your offspring's estimation so why not be yourself? We encourage young people not to be influenced by others but to develop their own opinions. Surely parents have that right too.

So, having cleared all the debris out of the way, what do you find you can really have in common with your kids? Who cares whether Busted, Stevie Wonder, Coldplay or Pink Floyd take the musical biscuit. Everyone to their own in matters of style, what we do with our free time and which direction our baseball caps are facing. Here are some alternative suggestions. Do you like one another's company? Both enjoy new experiences? Laugh at least at some of the same things. Aspire to something more than just the material world. Get frustrated with the flannel, self serving and distortion of politics. Think that something can and should be done about farmers who find the only way they can make a living is to grow marijuana. If you can agree about some of that – or whatever else you both think really matters in the world - then the rest shouldn't cause too much disagreement. And if you should grow to love the tuneful Busted by accident - don't let me stop you…

There's aye some bally thing however hard you try

– or is there?

"There's aye some bally thing however hard you try!" Along with a few other gems of frustration, this has gone down in my wife's family history as one of her late Dad's favourite war cries. And it's frequently repeated by all and sundry throughout the family whenever the occasion allows. Picture the scene. After months of delaying tactics, avoidance, and downright laziness you've finally galvanised yourself into action to fix that window / tap / shelf / hoover or. You've bought all the bits, hunted high and low till you've found the tools you need, set aside however long you think it might take, taken a deep breath and finally you're ready to go. Less than 2 minutes into whatever the grand repair you've stripped the bolt / broken the part / ladled your thumb with the hammer / dropped the moulded plastic fitting down the eaves or otherwise mucked it up. Besides that you've probably cut yourself, ripped your favourite shirt, broken the screwdriver and may even have smashed some other fitting or appliance that didn't need any attention at all.

So what's your reaction to this? After the regulation spitting and (possibly) swearing, you sit back and ponder that there is indeed always some bally thing however hard you try. And the harder you try the more bally things arise to frustrate and hinder. It's as if the universe has a regulation amount of chaos and disorder in it and any attempt to reduce the total is countered by physical laws to prevent you succeeding. So you may indeed manage to paint the shed today (after being unable to find the right brush, buying another at twice the price then finding the first exactly where you thought you'd previously looked for it) but nevertheless nature will bite back and reveal that the floorboards and roof are rotten and the shed needs replacing altogether. Like love, disorder will always find a way and that way usually runs clean counter to whatever you are trying to do.

It's like the old seafarer who comes back into his favourite inn after a five year absence with a wooden leg, an eye patch and a hook and the barman says,
"Welcome home Bill. But I see you've been in the wars. What happened to your leg?"

"Ah…," says Bill. "The wooden leg. Yes, that were a great sea battle when I lost the leg."

"Too bad," says the barman "so – how did you lose your hand?"

"Oh," says Bill, "that was a great storm at sea, and mast came down and pinned me arm. They had to cut me hand off to get it free. That's how I got this 'ere hook."

"That's rough," says the barman, "So what about your eye, how did you lose that?"

"Oh," says Bill. "That was before I got properly used to the hook…"

Life holds many traps for the unwary. And we do get the feeling that it's almost personal. Misfortune and blunder lie subdued but ever watchful until you try to do something that involves that extra effort and concentration. Then it all goes wrong. And like toddlers at nursery we moan, "That's not fair. I didn't deserve this!"

Well, if you feel like that you probably do have a point. It would be hard to prove that you really, genuinely did deserve to find the rotten timbers just after the paint on the shed was dry. Or to find that having sat up till 2.00 am finishing your report that the printer was out of ink. Or whatever. Nothing you have done in life has actually made it fair that these frustrating things should happen. But just before you relax with that, there might be a few other things you also didn't deserve…

Maybe you didn't deserve to see a fabulous sunrise this morning that you caught by accident on your way to the loo in the night. Or you didn't deserve to meet someone new, interesting and very attractive last month, have them agree to come out with you and now be head over heels in love. Or to catch a rerun of classic "Steptoe and Son" on the telly last night (even better - it was the one about the water bed) that had you in stitches all the rest of the evening. And there's the even more disturbing thought that as well as lots of good things you don't deserve (that you have got) there are also bad things you do deserve (that you haven't).

So the next time you break the only drill bit that'll fit or lock your keys in the car when it's time to run the kids to school, don't just spit and swear. Remember, there's always some beautiful thing – however hard you try.

Worry? I almost turned the telly off!

Two or three nights ago our two teenage boys were a bit late home from a weekend outing. It probably only takes about 45 minutes overdue for caring and appropriately anxious parents to start conjuring up a list of violent, immoral and physically traumatic events which might have delayed their offspring's return. As it happens we were watching a video of the Pelican Brief and didn't notice the time, so it was fully half twelve before we cottoned on and thought we maybe ought to start worrying. Where were they? Floating face down in the harbour perhaps. Or waiting to be treated in accident and emergency. Possibly captured by a party of hen nighting females and made to play Ann Summers games till they died of embarrassment (maybe a bit of retrospective wish fulfilment there I grant you).

In the event my wife texted the grown-ups in charge, found out they had been to a beach barbecue (no – really they had - in Orkney - this summer…), were currently getting lifts organised and since there was somebody coming out to the West Mainland anyway, should be home in about 20 minutes. It's the school holidays. They've got nothing to get up for tomorrow. They'll be home soon. No problem. Thanks.

This process of dawning realisation, doubt, slight concern, deepening anxiety, nervous trauma, out and out panic eventually followed by blasé reassurance and finally troubled sleep (punctuated by nightmares), has probably been going strong since our forbears huddled round the fire in Skara Brae, looked out at the state of the tide and thought, "Surely the kids should have been home by now!" It's in the nature of parenthood. Do expectant couples realise that they are putting their souls in hock the minute the little treasures pop out? From now on it's no longer even remotely up to you when you can sit back and relax and when you'll be panicking and phoning doctors, dentists, polis, fire brigade and possibly vets, plumbers and locksmiths too. The day our youngest drove down the stairs on his Noddy Car and had to have 7 teeth out will live in infamy.

All in all, it goes with the territory. They've got you just where they want you with no hope of time off for good behaviour. In fact the better

7

behaved you are the more likely you are to worry. Which of us doesn't slightly envy the apparently calm and untroubled state of mind enjoyed by the parents of 10 year old toe rags still wandering the streets at half past eleven at night (and school tomorrow) without an apparent care in the world. "Good parents" on the other hand worry themselves sick and hope the end result is worth it.

Which reminds me of a conversation I remember having as a fourteen year old with a bunch of pals at school. The subject was the worst row you've ever had. Each of us in turn tried to top the preceding tale of murder and mayhem which our parents had found out about and responded to with the emotional equivalent of the mushroom cloud. Bob Armstrong was (I think) the winner with the story of how he and his younger brother were battling on the stairs with quasi medieval weapons. Swords were apparently too tame so he got hold of a stretcher pole from the washing line and launched it at younger sibling at that point making a determined assault on the upper floor. Said sibling noticed its approach and understandably took evasive action. A split second later both were treated to the happy sounds of shattering glass as the stretcher went rocketing through the plate glass window at the foot of the stairs. I suppose Mr. and Mrs. Armstrong were left wondering when they got home whether they should be furious that the stretcher missed their beloved offspring and melted the plate glass window or whether they would have preferred it to be stopped before the window and impale their son who would probably mend without the services of a glazier. Ahhh. Back then it was awesome admiration of the scale of row attained. I see it a wee bit differently now…

So anyway, what's to be done about it? I mean this constant feeling of impending disaster that goes skulking about the parental subconscious? While it rarely gets to the point of children speared with garden implements and plate glass windows in fragments you always feel it could if you turn your back too long. As with much else in life the options are rather limited. Either leave your feelings in the freezer or get used to it. Caring about anyone strangely does involves care in its strictest sense. Things could be a whole lot neater, cleaner and less uncertain with no-one to care about. Also terminally dull and ultimately pointless. In an age that seems to be bent on removing risk wherever possible, a risk assessment prior to parenthood is only a matter of time. And what would it show? Hazards? Everywhere and at all times. Risks? Broken arms, legs, hearts and windows. Outcome – go ahead anyway. Obviously.

Forget computers, phones and faxes

– at last some technology you really need…

I recently heard some survey results about what people consider the most important inventions of the 20th Century. All the usual candidates were up there – TV, computers, mobile phones (of course), fibre optics, satellites, jet aircraft, the Internet, etc., etc. All very interesting and helpful but what I'm interested in are things that haven't been invented yet but should have been. Just imagine how life could be different with a few simple changes…

First of all, picture the scene. It's the office party / neighbourhood barbecue / Auntie Jessie's 80th birthday / 2nd cousin Billy's eldest daughter's wedding. Whatever. Suddenly you find yourself being advanced upon by a formidable looking lady about to greet you as her nearest and dearest. You, on the other hand, don't have a clue who she is except that her dress reminds you a bit of the Flintstones and her hairdo of something you saw in Petmania. Never fear - the Loose Talk Name-a-Tron to the rescue. Using a miniature camera concealed in the leg of your bifocals, linked to a computerised database in the soles of your Hush Puppies and a speech synthesizer disguised as a hearing aid (ok – doubling as a hearing aid), you get the low down whispered in a choice of voices (current bestseller Kelly Le Brock).
"Psst. It's Daphne from the charity shop. You bought the jacket you're wearing there last County Show weekend. Big Jim Reeves fan. Used to live next door to Uncle Bob and Aunt Lily. She fancies you y'know!" With the help of this vital advance warning, you are able to smile serenely, zoom off to the bar and engage in a much more interesting conversation: ("Tracy from Accounts. Last year's Christmas Party. Likes Bon Jovi, moonlit walks and swimming with dolphins. Good sense of humour. Non smoker. Buy her a Babycham!" Clearly useful for blokes with age related memory loss – meaning all of us.

Next up, technology to the rescue for another perennial problem. If I say "Has anyone seen my glasses / wallet / car keys / book / corkscrew?" you'll know where we're going with this one. Not that technology hasn't had a go already. Anyone else out there got the whistle sensitive key fob from the Innovations Catalogue? You know the routine. Lost the car keys? Kids need to be in school in three minutes flat? No problem. Just give a little whistle and your every helpful key fob will start chirping back from wherever it may be lurking. Of course this does mean running round the house like a demented burglar whistling madly in every single room and listening out for a cheerful reply. Then when you finally do get the right response you've got to track it down. This involves hurling cushions, magazines and discarded clothing into the air while groping recklessly down the sides of the sofa. All you find down there of course is old toast and apple cores at which point you tell the kids to walk and slump exhausted in the corner.

My solution is simpler. Instead of responding to your answering whistles once already lost, I propose something to stop essential objects getting lost in the first place. So in the Cowan house of the future any item laid down where it shouldn't go or not returned to its proper berth within a reasonable space of time will emit a loud piercing squeal until the offending household member picks it up and puts it where it should go! All domestic items would come with household location systems as standard and have quick and simple set up routines NOT using the Windows operating system. Of course it might be simpler if housemates simply put things back where they should go but we all know that's never going to happen.

Finally, my last suggestion is prompted by this morning's freezing cold shower. No, that's not part of my normal daily health routine but results from (I think) the hot water tank immerser packing in. Hence I propose that all future electrical appliances be fitted with predictive breakdown indicators. What's the point in finding out something doesn't work once it's already broken down! Even I can work that one out. I want to know when it's going to give up the ghost so I can get another, have it serviced or plan to eat out that night – not start the day with a shower that would have Scott of the Antarctic hopping about and howling for help.

So, for next year's Science Festival I propose the Loose Talk Award for sensible science and technology you can trust. All patents become the property of this column and profits go to therapy for aging technophobes who can't remember names, can never find their glasses and don't know how to fix the shower. You know it makes sense.

If I ruled the world...

"As any skoolboy kno..." we live in an increasingly regulated society. Just about anything you do that has any public or social dimension seems to be hedged round with laws, regulations, stipulations and ordinances. New car and home ownership are a minefield for the unwary, planning rules seem to be about as bewildering for the controlled as the controlling and owning and running a business needs masses of form filling long before you ever hang a roll of wallpaper, service a tractor or bill your first day's life coaching consultancy. No doubt all of this is as it should be and there are good reasons why things need to be properly done. Nevertheless sometimes it seems this barrage of law might be missing its target.

A few months ago we all got our voter's roll update forms. I am of course delighted to be able to fill these in, particularly since so many people around the world continue to risk harassment, beatings and imprisonment for that very privilege. Nevertheless the form makes it plain that failure to fill it in correctly is a criminal offence. Not a rap on the knuckles and "go away and do it right". Not ticking the right boxes is dealt with by the same legal code as if I were to burrow into next door's living room and make off with their DVD player. Whether anyone ever gets banged up to rights for it is beside the point. That's what might happen if you leave it stuffed behind the clock with all other official missives and warnings.

This set me thinking about things that really should be against the law. You know – the things that really get your goat - if you have any goat left to be got. While our worthy lawmakers are properly occupied with standing committees, derogations, subsidiaries and third readings, what is it that drives their subjects round the twist and would most easily make for a happier and more humane society...

Pondering my top three candidates for "New Law of the Year – 2006" I have shuffled through masses of candidates, duly weighted the pros and cons, cost/benefit analysed way past bed time and eliminated many worthy but not quite irritating enough potential additions. For example "Overuse of the word 'Like'" stood a good chance for a while. You know the sort of thing. "I was like... and she was like... so together we were like… y'know…" It's not widely known that the editors of the Oxford English Dictionary issue all English words with a currency counter and, once exceeded, the word in question has be struck from the list and can't be used again until it's recovered. I still hope in years to come to tell my nearest and dearest I really like her new perfume / dress / pay rise or exciting new ways with chicken tonight but if poor overused "like" has to go into a couple of years of retirement I might not be able to! Similarly "Spurious use of Statistics" was a likely contender until 46% of those questioned didn't agree, 33% did and the remaining 21% preferred to ban all pointless surveys.

So what have we got? New Loose Talk Law Number One is – "Failure to properly tighten screw top lids on liquid containers" You know exactly what I mean. You unsuspectingly pick up a tasty jar of baby beets in vinegar (by the lid), get it about six inches off the table when "crash!", table cloth, carpet and shirt front are instantly a fetching shade of pink while you are left with the lid in your hand, howls of amusement or ridicule all around the table and yourself foaming at the mouth in powerless rage.

Number Two may be particularly close to the heart of northerners trying to get back from south so as not to see their ferry of choice steaming happily homeward leaving them on the pier. The secret to this is of course the simple expedient – leave on time! However roadworks, toilet stops, flat tyres and lorry spray can sometimes knock the most cautious of schedules out the window. These are unavoidable. What is avoidable (and should be outlawed) are drivers plodding along the single carriageway sections of the A9 at a steady 45 (nothing in itself wrong with that) until they hit the duel carriageway, then shoot up to 75 making sure nobody except sales reps in BMWs can get by then, when the central reservation peters out, slink back to a stately 45 again. Can you feel the frustration even reading about it?

Finally, a word for that fine and much maligned body of men and women – the national weather forecasters. And this is not a complaint about wrong, dismal, incomprehensible or even badly mapped weather forecasts. It's about that galling opening line, "And for tonight's forecast, I'm going to start with central and southern parts of England, South Wales, East Anglia and everything south of the Pennines. Ahhhhh! Night after night. If you live further north than Macclesfield they make you wait till all the important people have had their weather first then you get a wee bit tacked on at the end. No doubt they'll tell us it's so we always know when our bit is coming up – after everybody else. But that's like saying we're going to let the girls in first to school dinners every single day of the year so the boys always know when it's their turn - after the steak pie's all finished and there's only cottage cheese and bagels left. Just now and again I'd like to know what the weather might be doing before my limited attention span has fizzled out, I've lost concentration and missed the bit I've been waiting half and hour to hear.

So there we go. Not a lot to ask is it? And the next time you hear a knock on the door from a political canvasser while you're cleaning up the beetroot juice, trying to catch the weather forecast or wondering if your family will make it home tonight, see if they can get that in the manifesto.

Victor we need you now!

If TV sums up popular culture these days (and who would doubt it) what would you say are the signature TV themes of the new millennium? You know, the small screen moments that sum up how people are feeling and where the nation is going. Perhaps it might be the reality shows. Housemates, cooks, singers, dancers, castaways, fat slobs, almost everyone vying for a place in the nation's affections and phone bills. (By the way, would you say a Vote of reality show contestants or maybe an Eviction?) Or perhaps the lifestyle stream. After a hard day in the office, what is it you most want to do? Put that Gin and Tonic down and get ready to do your back out in the garden or fall off a ladder with a strip of freshly pasted wallpaper wrapped around you.

Those who live anywhere near me will not be surprised to hear that my reality vote goes to Grumpy Old Men. Fifty glorious minutes of bad tempered blokes frothing at the mouth about things that frankly don't matter. Nobody mentions climate change, third world debt or inner city delinquency. No, it's all super market trolleys, self assembly furniture and computers. Anything about computers. From the packaging to the ads to the way it mucks up your system without so much as a by-your-leave to that demented dog that appears from nowhere to say, "It looks like you're writing a column for Orkney Today. Can I help you with that?" "No you cannot! Leave me alone. Go back to the fifth dimension of cyberspace where you belong and never darken my screen again!" Incidentally, after introducing that whole hellish family of animated helpers, the largest class of technical help calls Microsoft got was from computer users at their wits end trying to get rid of them. Restores your faith in humanity doesn't it..?

So anyway, why Grumpy Old Men? In an age where it seems like we've never had it so good (incomes, choice, life expectancy, opportunity and travel at least, if not the weather), why are we so collectively grumpy? And why do we so enjoy anyone else giving voice to our own low level rumbles of discontent? Well maybe, as you will all know when you expected a racer for Christmas and got the Blue Peter Annual, it's not what you've got, it's what you thought you were going to get that really counts. Forty and fifty somethings (among whom I proudly number myself) have all been brought up to expect the world to get relentlessly better. Science fiction telly in our formative years had the cast bouncing around in outfits made of bacofoil, eating protein pills, going to Mars for their holidays, working (if at all) via viewscreen and visiting your pals by hovercar. What we've got are incurable bugs you pick up in hospital, students leaving college with on average over £9,000 worth of debt and nagging doubts about the honesty of our leaders (maybe no change there of course). It has been said that the best form of government is dictatorship moderated by assassination. Makes you think dunnit?

So, in the spirit of a good old moan that will never have any effect on anything, can I propose the Victor Meldrew Awards for Things We Didn't Expect and Shouldn't Have to Put Up With. It's been a close run thing for this year's (inaugural) award and this column is delighted to announce the winners. In the category "Risk to Life and Limb", we have shower controls that vary between bone chillingly freezing and hotter than molten porridge in less than one degree of turn. In the new category "Relentless and Pointless Sales Calls" we have companies offering mains gas supplies in Orkney. (I've often been tempted to sign up then complain when the fitter fails to appear). And finally, this year's grand award is a group winner awarded unanimously to "Adverts that Make no Sense". While the judges did try their best to sort out an individual winner, it turns out to be beyond the powers of concentration to separate one of these visually stunning, thematically incomprehensible non-entities from another. Stallions merging into pounding surf, forest fires and glaciers, 3D flythroughs in complex and fantastic virtual environments. None of us has a clue what products we are supposed to love or hate, but at least it makes you appreciate a darkened room and the G 'n' T I put down to do the gardening. Grumpy? You bet I am but I hope to feel better fairly soon.

Ding, Ding, Seconds Out

- Round One in the bathroom arena

Good morning viewers and welcome to the bathroom arena. Today's bout comes to you as part of the "Getting Ready for Work" series and features the regular bill - you've seen it all before but every contest brings its own surprises. Who knows what the outcome could be. First off it's the fat baldy bloke in the red underpants versus Mr. Gillette who this morning is wearing an all over chrome finish and a wide shiny grin. The crowd are as excited as ever with the series so far running quite close at 3,784 to 4,592. Needless to say there's a few out there frankly looking for blood.

So here we go. The fat baldy bloke seems in quite a lather with Mr. Gillette looking as sharp as ever. They're getting close and – yes - there it is. First stroke and the fat bloke comes away with a clean left cheek and no visible injuries. Now it's Gillette who's looking a bit lathered up. Not such a bright smile now! The crowd is tense and quiet. Suddenly a heckler's voice is heard from the changing rooms.
"Will you get a move on in there? It's half past eight!"
Things move up a gear now. Second, third and fourth strokes are quick and even. Left cheek now completely clear including the jaw line and the tricky bit up under the ear lobe. Everything seems to be going the fat bloke's way, but Gillette's not finished yet. He gets a good dowsing under the cold tap. That should wake him up a bit. Odds on the fat bloke throwing in the towel.

Now the right side gets a good doing. Gillette still cutting an absolute swathe through the defence and coming up ready for more. Coaches will be pleased with the way the new triple blade, easy action, bend and flex system is bearing up. But fat bloke seems to be coping well with the pressure and looks increasingly good as the bout goes on. There's that heckler again.
"The kids need to be out in five minutes. Ok???"
Fat bloke speeds up and looks like he's on the final curve. But what's that? Gillette pulls out a sharp right uppercut and there's the blood. Fat bloke is swearing and reaching for the toilet roll. Today's result: Gillette

one, fat bloke nil. The fight was stopped in the first round with a cut to the lower right side. Seconds are being called in.

"I've cut myself again. Can you wait a minute?"

"Well hurry up. I've still to do my teeth!!!"

Ok – so that's an exaggeration but sometimes getting out the door in the morning can sometimes feel like a fight to the finish. Men do battle with the razor and wear exactly the same thing they wore yesterday while women apparently have the daily problem of not under any circumstances being able to wear the same thing they had on the day before. And then there's getting the kids up, dressed, fed, packed, equipped for gym, remembering their school bags, hunched over maths homework on the school run and told to phone if they're going to be late. And all of that's before the day has really begun. The traumas you face at work can be as nothing compared with the logistics of that early morning hour between the first cheery strains of Wake up to Wogan and tearing out the door with seconds to spare. Apparently there are people who start each day with 15 minutes gentle yoga, an uplifting daily reading or half an hour over the hill with the dogs. I am not one of them. Ever since having to get up at twenty past six every morning from age 13 to 18 to deliver papers before school (and one evening a week), I've treated every extra moment in bed as only reasonable recompense.

On the other hand, it does seem such a shame. The early morning hour can be the best of the day. If you get up early enough it's the one time you're guaranteed no interruptions. It's the mental equivalent of one last deep breath before plunging into activity, assertiveness, ongoing performance appraisal and juggling the dozen different demands every day holds. Why add to the stress with the domestic equivalent of an Aldershot assault course. So here's the Loose Talk recipe for a gentler, easier start to the day.

GET OUT OF BED ON TIME YOU LAZY LUMP!

Apricot Jam? You must be joking!

Some years ago we had the chance to visit a former work colleague of my wife's living at that time near Los Angeles. With a name like Liz Taylor (her name not mine) you do expect special treatment and we weren't disappointed being introduced to the fantastic American custom of "going out for breakfast". "Lulu's" was the venue and the grub, it has to be said, did make you want to shout – in the nicest possible way. Besides all the routine fried fare included in any full Scottish / English / Irish / Welsh breakfast (what is the difference?), otherwise known as "heart attack on a plate", the menu had such appealing delicacies as "Scrambled eggs with avocados" and "Smoked salmon omelette with chives".

All was going splendidly until in an exchange that will live in infamy, I innocently inquired about the one missing ingredient. Now, as most Brits, and absolutely all Scots know a slice of toast is seriously underdressed without a liberal spread of tasty, tangy marmalade. And no substitute will do. Imagine my horror then on being told (what, you're kidding, I don't believe it) "Sorry. We don't have any marmalade". Stunned silence... Embarrassed pause from waitress... Feeble attempt to remedy situation… "I can get you some Apricot jam…"

Well, in true ex-pat fashion we made the best of the situation. We declined the apricot jam with proper disdain, finished our avocados in gloomy silence, trashed the joint and left for our next appointment with Americana – three miles of power walking round a desolate field laughingly called a park, followed by tap dancing roller skaters on Venice Beach. Still, somehow I wasn't able to fully enjoy it all. Breakfast toast with no marmalade. Ah me…

So apart from making me the breakfast guest from hell, what's the point of all this? Is the lack of breakfast marmalade a portent of worse to come. First there's no marmalade then law and order start breaking down. Before we know it dogs and cats are living together, holiday makers are coming to Orkney for the climate and all the norms of life are overturned. Well, clearly not but despite that there is a point. Simply this, there's no accounting for taste.
I like marmalade as probably do most of you. Americans by and

large (it appears) don't. My Dad liked a chunk of Danish Blue on cream crackers. Like people with an allergy for nuts, even a whiff of the horrendous stuff made me feel the need for medical attention. I like science stuff on the telly which bores my spouse to tears. Some kids could watch pop videos for Queen and Country, of which I could probably stand about 30 seconds. I like an obscure prog rock band called Camel which they would probably find intensely dull. Etc. etc.

So there's no accounting for taste, and likes and dislikes are important, sometimes to the point of obsession. Be it music, football teams, politics, where you live or a thousand other things. For many of us the things we like and dislike are inseparable from who we are and pity help those that take another view. I have seen erstwhile pals almost come to blows over whether Queen were the best rock band ever or not. What football fans do to each other week by week is well documented.

So what's the alternative? On the one hand we could all end up easy-oasy, take it or leave it, whatevers. That way everybody would be ok with whatever they got which I grant you could probably make a great many of us a whole lot easier to get on with. The downside of course is that nobody much cares about anything so nobody goes to any effort to make things the way they should be. Imagine Delia in the kitchen. "Oops. The hollandaise seems to have curdled. Oh well. Never mind. Anyway, over here we're just waiting for the duchesse potatoes to brown up nicely. Oh dear. Several of them seem to have burned to a cinder. Well, that's just the way I like them." Or Jeremy Clarkson on Top Gear. "I have to say the new Mercedes is overpriced, underpowered, ugly to look at and hopeless to drive. But that's ok with me…"

Perhaps it would be better for everyone to be enthusiastic enough about what they like – just so long as we all like the same things. In fact this seems to be precisely what mass marketing is aiming to achieve anyway. Everybody should drink the same drinks, wear the same clothes, go to the same places on holiday, drive the same cars and like the same kind of music. On second thoughts that sounds even worse. Nothing but soaps to watch, Ronan Keating to listen to, Ibiza on holiday and turkey dinosaurs for tea.

So what's to be done about it? Painfully, reluctantly, finally, it seems there's no alternative. No matter how appalling my taste in music, menswear or marmalade you'll just have to put up with it. And I'll have to do the same with your taste for Jim Reeves, reality TV and raspberry jam. C'est la vie, que sera sera, vive la difference and any other expressions you think fit the bill.

Just don't be surprised if I don't take you up on the offer of apricot jam.

Take it or leave it, it's magic!

Growing up in Falkirk district didn't have many advantages –
None of the gallus swagger of Glasgow, the arts and culture of
Edinburgh, the beauty of the Highlands or the history and interest of a
place like Orkney. Most of the year in fact not much but foundries on their
last legs, a not very fantastic football team ("Wilson, Oh Wilson Hogan,
Wilson Hogan on the wing") and a couple of Victorian institutions for
those they thought were better locked away. However, over one week
in October we had the famous, historical and, to a child's imagination,
absolutely magical Falkirk Tryst Fair.

The Tryst began life as a horse and cattle fair, grew to include lots of
other things including entertainment for the traders, then as the livestock
faded away, all that remained was the fair. Same patch of waste ground
half way up Tryst Road (where else), same week of the year and same
mixture of stalls, rides, mud and full volume pop hits blasting out from
the Waltzers and the Chair-o-Planes - usually "Nutbush City Limits" as I
remember it. Same gaggles of teenage girls and guys eyeing each other
up over the Jungle Ride. Same mixture of noise, smoke, flashing lights,
terror, excitement, nausea and over all an indefinable, overwhelming air
of mystery and excitement..

Sure it was full of stall holders intent on parting you and your money as
quickly as possible with the aid of a set of air rifles with their barrels bent
so it took you three goes to get the right aim, rides that made you throw
up, machinery that last saw a health and safety inspector (if at all) on
its way out the factory gates and all sorts of unsavoury characters we
wouldn't want our daughters to bring home to Sunday lunch. But still,
it was fantastic to a child's imagination. The mixed up smells of diesel
fumes, candy floss, chips and vinegar. The lurid figures painted on the
walls of the rides, the deafening roar of the attractions merging together
as you drifted between the Divebombers, the Rib Tickler, the Ghost
Train and the Carousel. The varied sounds and expressions as toddlers
were hurled round in push chairs either mesmerised by the whole thing
or greeting heartily in terror. It was undoubtedly a mixed bag but what a
fantastic mix!

As well as all the magic on open show however, there was also magic wrapped in mystery. Either because you couldn't afford it, weren't old enough or your Dad wouldn't let you, there were certain places you couldn't go. Stalls that advertised the World's Strongest Man, The Bearded Lady, The Inseparable Twins, the Wild Man of Borneo, The Egyptian Mummy, Reptile Man and (most off limits of all) What the Butler Saw. Sometimes however, on the way past, you could sneak half a glimpse into the tent if a fully paid up visitor was going through and held up the curtain for a second or two. What you saw was little enough but it was added to by your imagination until you thought you had seen something fantastic, hidden, and full of secret significance.

Maybe all very interesting, you might be thinking, but not a very festive theme. What's all that got to do with holly and mistletoe and Santa and presents. Well, my annual visit as the Falkirk Tryst Fair seems to me now quite a lot like Christmas.

Of course it's a rip off, it's commercial, it's bright lights and noise, it's too much to eat and drink, it's feeling distinctly queasy afterwards, it's unsavoury in the extreme as well as full of glitter and glamour and possibly even goldfish. On the other hand, it's also chock full of magic. It's kids (and grown ups) with faces full of excitement hardly able to believe their eyes. It's beautiful and unexpected and fun and fanciful and a roller coaster of emotions.

Besides these however, fun as they are, it can also be a glimpse of something more. Like when the curtain is pulled aside for a fraction of a second to hint at something deeper, more mysterious and more fundamental – if you're interested enough to have a look. What you think might lie inside that particular tent I can't say. Many believe however that rather than being merely a sideshow, this mystery may be the main event of human affairs. And like anything important, you won't take it all in at first glance – you'll have to look deeper and closer in.

So whether your Christmas anthem this year is "Once in Royal David's City", "Happy Christmas, War is Over" or even "So here it is Merry Christmas, everybody's having fun", you might want to have a look under the curtain this year. You never know what you might find…

The Lion, the Witch, the Wardrobe

... and the critics

Mrs. Forbes, primary five teacher at Larbert Village Primary School, loved to read to her class and they in turn loved to be read to at the end of a taxing day of nouns, verbs and hard sums. I can say this with some confidence having been a member of that class for all too short a year. So it was we were introduced to Stig of the Dump, Smith (the Victorian pickpocket), Long John Silver and the Quest for the Eagle of the Ninth. At the end of every schoolday - if we'd been good and got our work done - jotters, textbooks and pencils were put away, desks cleared, the blackboard wiped, paints and stencils removed, the Reading Lab restored to order and out came the book of the moment. Amazingly, silence would almost always reign and we'd sit spellbound, transported into other lands, ages and lives.

One story among all others stood out even then however and I think I still have a pretty clear memory of what it was about. Four children find their way through a magical wardrobe into a new and exciting land of giants, dwarfs, centaurs, fauns and talking beasts. As well as being pulled into this new mysterious kingdom, they were also pulled into the war between the White Witch who makes it always winter and never Christmas, and Aslan the great Lion who has come to restore order and bring back the spring. Despite all of Aslan's powers however, he cannot win the war alone and needs the children to fulfil the old prophesy by participating in the battle so eventually they can sit on the four thrones at Cair Paravel by the sea. Events take a disastrous turn however as Aslan's army is betrayed by Edmund - one of the four - which brings Aslan to the point of giving his own life to rescue Edmund and reunite the children. Magnificently however, he doesn't stay dead and comes back to life again by virtue of the "deep magic". Together, they go on to defeat the White Witch and restore peace and freedom to the land of Narnia. It was a fabulous story and kept us riveted to our seats, utterly spellbound until that day's installment was over.

There was one problem however. Either due to lack of attention or perhaps being poked at the crucial moment by Bobby Rae or George Penman (both likely and frequent offenders), I did pick up that the book was called "The Lion, the Witch and the Wardrobe" but missed the name of the author and worst of all the fact that there were six other stories in the series involving other adventures in Narnia. Hence for the next five years I had only the memory of a wonderful story set in a magical land but without a clue as to how to find the book again and utterly ignorant that there may have been other things that also happened there. It was as if the wardrobe had not only been locked but stuck on a removal lorry and trundled off to storage never to be found again.

At the age of about 15 however a new pal invited me round to his house and there - amazingly - stuck on the bedroom wall was a map in greens, yellows and browns entitled "The Chronicles of Narnia." What?!? Not only Narnia but Chronicles - plural. As I recall, it fairly quickly dawned that this meant more than one. Other stories. Other characters. More about Aslan the Lion. Now you may be thinking "What's a 15 year old doing jumping up and down over a children's fairy tale when he ought to be rocking to Neil Young or chilled out to Cat Stevens?" Well, in my own defence I was doing a bit of that too, but there was something about Aslan and Narnia that sent a shiver up the spine and tingled in the imagination. I begged the complete set and, it being almost the Easter holidays, knocked off the entire series within the next ten days. It absolutely lived up to expectations. In subsequent years I have read them to our boys, reread them for my own pleasure and pondered their meaning and impact.

I'm not sure at what point the real "deep magic" of Narnia finally bobbed up as it became clear who Aslan actually was. C. S. Lewis, author of the Narnia stories and many other both serious and imaginative works has said that Aslan does not represent Christ as (for example) Faithful represents loyalty and persistence in The Pilgrim's Progress. Rather, Aslan is as Christ might be in another world and saves that world and its inhabitants in a manner appropriate to them as he has in this world in a manner appropriate to us. Once you catch hold of that handle, other characters, events and comments in the story take on an even richer, deeper significance.

And therein lies the rub. The Narnian stories have a Christian background and critics hostile to feeling that their imaginations have been hijacked in such a way have laid into the books over the years with accusations as varied as misogyny, middle class cosiness, and principally as being spiritual propaganda. The recent Disney film which has played to sell out houses at the Picky cinema has of course added to the angst since it exposes another generation to the offending material in an even more powerful and immediate way. The children's author Philip Pullman has described the film as "devoid of Christian virtue". Left wing critics have likened the war against the Witch to the war in Iraq and seen it as a covert attempt by the US media to show our boys as on the side of God and all others as fit only for destruction. Richard Dawkins in his recent TV series refers to religion as "a virus we pass on to our children" of which "The Lion, the Witch and the Wardrobe" would no doubt be exhibit A.

So how should we feel about this point of view? Maybe there's is a clue in my reaction to the story long before I had any idea what else it might refer to - likewise in its sell out status at the Picky. Principally, these are tales of heroism, betrayal, self sacrifice and doing what you know to be right in the face of danger, ridicule and a sense of hopelessness. As children's stories they present a simpler view of the world and, as such, set aside many of the extenuating circumstances we so often apply to our own motives and actions. In Narnia there are no excuses, mitigations or get out clauses. Edmund's actions have to be paid for. As it happens, by another dying on his behalf. If you don't like Lewis's sources then think of it as the French Resistance or the doctor who contracts AIDS trying to save a patient's life. These are virtues of the highest order and much needed in a mealy mouthed age of mixed motives, "errors of judgement", peer pressure and "economy with the truth". Surely we need all the help we can get to illuminate that some things are simply right and wrong and should be treated accordingly. And by the way we might find things working in reverse as well, as Narnia throws its own light on stories we've known since childhood in a new and magical way.

Three Cheers for Exams?

There musht be shome mishtake…

There was a time when fathers could shout up the stairs "Turn that electric guitar off and get on with your revision!" No more. In fact nowadays "that electric guitar" is revision. Along with the keyboard, bass and drums (spare a thought for the neighbours), causes and possible culprits of the Kennedy assassination, uses of spreadsheets and databases, the physics of health care, the chemistry of brewing (theory only) and characters and plot in Catch 22.

How many men it takes to dig a hole, principal exports of New Zealand and Lear, Hamlet and Falstaff seem to have vanished without trace. And maybe a good job too. It's probably too much to hope for that the exam curriculum should all be of practical use in life (I have yet to find a suitable slot for sin., cos. or tan. in the daily grind) but the nearer to relevant most can get, so much the better.

Maybe music is one of the clearest examples. For many of us music at school meant singing. Hymn singing. Hymn singing to an out of sorts piano played by a music teacher with a temperament to match. So much so that Bunyan's "hobgoblin or foul fiend" did have a strange relevance possibly never intended. As I recall though, "Stand up, Stand up for Jesus" resulted in seeing who could sit down longest without being spotted and "Onward Christian Soldiers" gave little needed encouragement to 3B to mime gunning down the school choir with a panache Rambo would have been proud of.

The thought that rock and pop would ever be part of the actual curriculum was beyond our wildest dreams. At that time if you wanted to learn guitar or drums you did so in spite of the gods of music teaching not because of them. Nowadays it may be accepted that Dark Side of the Moon was a work of genius and that Jimi was more a force of nature than just a rock guitarist. In those days both existed only in the outer darkness of the adolescent's record collection not the holy ground of the school curriculum.

Or Kennedy. Who shot him, why, where from and whether they've ever been brought to justice are questions most of us have pondered even to a slight extent at some time in the last 30 years. Now the whole train of events from the cavalcade through Dallas to the fatal gunshots, Lee Harvey Osward's arrest and subsequent murder by Jack Ruby, the role of the CIA, Cuban refugees and even Marilyn Monroe are all up for grabs (so to speak). Along the way young people learn to weigh evidence, consider likelihoods and come up with probabilities on the hunt for historical truth. Pretty relevant skills particularly during the run up to a UK general election some might say.

So when we hear about the exam curriculum being dumbed down and getting easier, perhaps it might be that some of the content is getting more relevant, more interesting and more likely to be some use in later life. Maybe this is a direct help to students as they study. Maybe being interested in what you have to learn does help you remember it and maybe for that reason more exam candidates do get better marks. And maybe it does nothing for young people's motivation at this time of year to tell them that even if they do well it's because it's not as hard as it used to be.

So I for one am happy to hear one particular exam candidate upstairs thrashing out guitar riffs, staying up late to watch "JFK" and laughing at the rude bits of Catch 22. At one time education was expected to be dull and struggling though King Lear and the Periodic Table was thought to put hairs on your chest and build powers of determination necessary for surviving a dull career. If kids are now learning cool stuff relevant to life and seeing the world in a new way, well at least two and a half cheers for exams.

And in the meantime, for the last time will you turn that electric guitar down!

Steady now…don't do anything rash…

How often have you thought of booking that holiday, buying that car, applying for that job, buying that house, engaging in a little harmless romance or retraining as a circus performer when stopped abruptly in your tracks by the relentless inner voice of Caution and Restraint. You want to do something rash and reckless, something without regard to the consequences, something that will leave all your friends, relations and co-workers gasping with amazement and not a little admiration. Instead you do the sensible thing and keep strictly on the straight and narrow. Your mad impulse to give life a slide tackle that'll teach it who's boss is interrupted by the referee of responsibility and the yellow card of common sense. Any more of that and you'll be off to an early bath my boy…

I call it the sensible shoes effect. Year after year you went with your Mum to the shoe shop just a few days before the start of the new school year with the forlorn hope that maybe this year you might get the wet look boots with 3 inch platforms and multicoloured laces you'd seen Slade wearing on Top of the Pops. And year after year you came home with standard issue, fit for purpose, boring, black, sensible shoes. This goes on for so long that even once you have the money and independence to buy whatever shoes you want, all the fight's gone out of you. Hush Puppies? That'll do nicely. What's that? Waterproofing spray and original colour restorer? Why not.

Well, if that's how you feel, Loose Talk comes this week to bring hope to the hopeless and a ray of sunshine to the terminally sensible. You see, recent research has discovered that as well as genetic inheritance from its parents, certain physical and mental powers and a good strong set of lungs, all children are endowed at birth with a lifetime allocation of reckless decisions. These do vary slightly from person to person depending on how reckless your parents have been in having you - County Show night babies appear to have had some of their allocation already used up - but nevertheless, we all have some, to do with as we wish in our own future lives. And like any worthwhile capital, what we don't use up can be kept for a rainy day and may even grow if well invested…

So if you've spent 30 or 40 years being sensible, just imagine how much you've got left! And as with rural post offices, the Use it or Lose it rules apply so maybe now's the time to start making a few withdrawals from the barmy bank. Where do you want to start? Regardless of what your spouse might say, we think you'd look good in a leather fringe jacket or orange dungarees. And don't forget the platform boots. Why not take up the saxophone or drums? Learn Esperanto. Do a degree in Pink Floyd (there's bound to be one). Send your poetry to the papers. Dye your hair pink, decorate your wedding suit with safety pins and move to Alicante. Finally determine that you will learn to juggle and you will tell Aunt Edith what to do with the next kitten calendar she sends you.

To be more serious however, how much human misery is caused by feeling we always have to live up to other people's expectations instead of doing what we've always dreamed of and weren't allowed to by Mum, Dad, the voice of reason or the bylaws. After about the age of 35 or so, the truth gradually dawns that life will not go on forever and there will not always be the chance to do at some undisclosed time in the future what we haven't had the energy, confidence or daring to have a go at to date. Much as this column despises multinational advertising, the Nike slogan "Just do it" does have something going for it. Sometimes that's all there is for it.

Now, of course, we're not actually saying you've got to get blootered in the park, abandon true friends for nutters, pack in your job to row around the world or take your Elvis impressions on the road. But the point is, life is far too short, or at least I expect mine to be, to put off forever what you know you'll regret never having tried. Sometimes the only safe thing to do is to take a risk. And you could start by clearing out your shoe cupboard and handing in a nice big bag of practical footwear to the Red Cross Shop. Can you still get platform boots and orange dungarees?

Harry Potter has an invisibility cloak for roaming around the grounds of Hogwarts after dark and solving mysteries or wreaking havoc. H.G. Wells created the character of Griffin "the most gifted physicist the world has ever seen" - better known as "The Invisible Man". The TV magician's vanishing act is amongst his most popular and any number of TV cartoons turn on what might happen when characters become invisible. Probably most of us have had the odd idle thought about what we might do and where we might go if we could be absolutely undetected. Some of these might even be printable…

For Wells' character however, invisibility was very soon revealed as a curse not a blessing. In small doses all very well but not so much fun when you've got it and can't get rid of it. Despite that however, the thought of being invisible does retain a bit of a fascination as one of these yearned after but pretty unlikely possible future discoveries. Maybe a bit like anti-gravity boots, diet pills and something to keep odd socks together.

It's a little known fact, however, that invisibility is actually pretty common and crops up all the time. Take teenagers' bedrooms for example. Although 3 weeks supply of used smalls may be perfectly visible to you - as well as being evident in other ways - to the youth concerned they are clearly absolutely invisible. Not a trace can they find. Nor can they find the laundry basket, while we're on the subject. Clean socks often turn out to be invisible as well of course, although this seems to be a less permanent state since waving them under the young person's nose sometimes can bring the item back into the visible spectrum. Particularly at about 8.30 am on a school day morning.

And to everyday dirty washing you could add homework assignments, dental appointments, the fiver they borrowed last week and promised to return as soon as pay day arrived and your "Best of the Who" CD spirited upstairs several months ago and now apparently no longer detectable by ordinary means.

Not to be "youth-ist" about this though, the same effect can apply throughout the family. It's often been said that men are incapable of finding a tub of marg in the fridge if the end that says "Margarine" isn't showing. The fact that the toilet roll has run out can be likewise beyond the apprehension for some of us. Car insurance renewal documents seem to slip out of visible light as soon as you open them and lay them down and as for my woolly hat and gloves, they seem to only have temporary visibility depending on the weather. Glorious sunshine and there they are, in my top drawer ready to be used at a moment's notice. As the thermometer drops they start to get a bit shaky round the edges and at anything less than 5 degrees or more than force 5 they're completely beyond detection.

What applies to inanimate matter also sadly applies to people, of course. Fall out with a friend and there's a good chance they may end up invisible, although early intervention and the ability to say that hardest word can render this a bit less likely. In some cases it doesn't even need the formal "falling out" event to produce the same effect. First you are bosom buddies, then old friends, then Christmas correspondents then mutually invisible.

To find your hat and gloves no longer in the visible dimension may be irritating, to lose sight of old friends can be a sadness but there are other things that are altogether more serious when they cease to be properly evident. Remember "Make Poverty History" and Gleneagles? The second of July was the first anniversary of the Edinburgh rally attended by almost a quarter of a million people in support of the campaign. Recent reports suggest that some of the targets everyone signed up to don't seem quite as solid now as they were back then. Over recent months events in South Lebanon also appear to have been pretty invisible to some…

Anyway, you get the idea. It takes an effort to give the people and things that really matter their proper focus. Things of absolutely no importance take up so much of our attention as if they were extra-visible. Maybe the trick is to tune them out and leave some bandwidth free for the big stuff. So while you are helping your teenager find their homework diary, raking up socks for wash day or trying to keep your car legally on the road, you can also remember to keep in touch, bother your MP from time to time and do that thing you know needs done and seems to be totally hidden to everyone else but you. At least that's what my invisible friend says. That right Harvey?

Two weeks in Marbella? Quiet you fool

- the tumble drier might be listening…

The summer's been and gone - apparently. Time for strawberries and cream, soaking up the sun (don't forget your factor 99 and the big floppy hat), pottering in the garden and of course Going on Holiday. What does the thought conjure up? In theory Going on Holiday is meant to be fun. The reality is somewhat different. We work away like beavers all winter, ferret away our savings, study the brochures till we're sick as parrots all to end up like headless chickens getting ready to catch the boat followed by 2 weeks basking like lizards on an overcrowded beach. Sounds like a dog's life to me…

Actually while much is said about the hassles of choosing a holiday everyone in the family will enjoy, the effort of getting ready for it and the disappointments of unfinished chalets and overcast skies, just to get the full traumatic effect we shouldn't neglect the final painful stage - home, sweet home. Amongst the mixture of post holiday emotions - usually a bit of regret at leaving just when you've found out where the supermercado and farmacia are and maybe even struck up a bit of Spanglish banter with the girl at reception - there is often at least a hint of relief at getting back to the devil we know. The post office, petrol station and Picky Centre are likely to be were you left them, work colleagues are just as delightful / bad tempered / co-operative / confusing / aimless or irritating as they were when you went away. And instead of spending a fortune on food you wouldn't eat for nothing you can get back to good, solid reliable home fare you know you can afford and might even enjoy.

But all is not sweetness and light however. Besides routine aggravations like a mountain of washing and rotten weather (it usually starts raining about Helmsdale when we come home), there is another not entirely predictable set of problems. Has anyone else noticed the surprising effect that when you get back from holiday Things Don't Work.

Despite switching all the switches and dialling the dials, the shower remains steadfastly stone cold and of course all plumbers and electricians are also on holiday. All battery operated appliances are totally flat and cost a fortune in double AAs to get working again. And as for the Internet… it's quite likely not to be working at all as your computer has taken advantage of your absence to change all settings and even if it is, all personal emails have been rudely bounced back from whence they came and instead you have 250 invitations to invest in dubious companies based in Nigeria or offers of on-line pharmaceuticals you are pretty sure nobody else should know you need.

Why is it? If humans are supposed to be distinguished from the animals by being the mighty toolmakers – well, getting back from holiday is Revenge of the Tools. They wait patiently all year then as soon as you take your eye off them for a couple of weeks they pounce and everything reverts to its basic state. Batteries are flat, water is cold and all communications have ceased.

So if that's the problem, what's the solution? Well this month Loose Talk proposes another boost to the service industries - technology sitting. It's like house-sitting but much less effort and much more benefit. Instead of guarding against burglars (unlikely), freezing pipes (even in Orkney, not a big risk in July) or subsidence (be realistic - what is the house-sitter supposed to do about it!), the technology sitter has an easy, do-able and even pleasant task. All it involves is fooling all house-technology into thinking you have decided not to go on holiday this year but instead are putting the money towards papering the back bedroom, saving an endangered species of plankton, your children's university education or some other pointless and ultimately doomed activity.

And for all the brains domestic appliances are supposed to have these days - like your washing machine having more computer power than took Armstrong and Aldrin to the moon (yeah…right) - this is actually quite easy to accomplish. All they need do is have a shower once a day, watch an hour or two of telly, pick up your email and poke about under the stairs with your rechargeable torch. Fantastic. And the clever bit is that even the appliances they don't use get the message. The tumble drier, dishwasher, alarm clocks and all seventeen hairdryers are convinced by the low level of background technology use that the most that may have happened is the wife has gone to her mother's for a bit and the kids are at holiday club. At least one technology user is remaining stubbornly at home keeping things ticking over and so they'll have to go on working for a bit yet.

And because it's so simple a single technology sitter can service an entire neighbourhood. The worst that can happen is that they end up very clean, overdosed on Emmerdale and party to all secret email sent by single girls from Basildon you met in the One2One chat room. Maybe not a bad price to pay for less of a bump to earth after next year's hard won two weeks in the sun. And don't forget Loose Talk Technology Sitting Services - where Quality Costs Less…

To Boldly Celebrate ...

...What None Have Celebrated Before

Did you miss it? If so, then you're probably not aware of it and wouldn't care anyway. If you didn't then you know exactly what I'm talking about and certainly think it was well worth celebrating. What was it? Well beam me up Scotty if Sept 8th this year wasn't the 40th anniversary of Star Trek! The TV series that boldly went where no series had gone before. The first black woman in a principal TV role, the first inter-racial kiss, the first use of warp drive and the first thing I used to watch on the telly every Friday night as soon as I got back from Scouts.

And as if to mark that anniversary in some eerie, more than coincidental way, friends who recently moved house and have been trying desperately to dump as much unwanted garbage as possible have just offloaded a box of 20 VHS tapes with about 80 episodes in total onto the Cowan household. While producing a feeling much like various birthdays and Christmases all coming at once, this is also threatening to turn me into even more of a couch potato than ever before. Or perhaps that should be Aldeberan Couch Turnip...

Probably the most successful TV franchise ever, certainly one of the most influential, Star Trek is a bit like what we used to be told about the British Empire. Apparently the sun never sets on Messrs Kirk, Spock, Picard and Janeway. Somewhere on earth someone is watching Star Trek every hour of the day and night. What a sad, solitary individual they must be...

And if that's what you are thinking, then you are not alone. Star Trek, as well as being hugely successful and influential over the years, has also been hugely parodied, scoffed at and ridiculed. The vision of Kirk rampaging round the galaxy, meeting funny coloured aliens and either blasting them to smithereens or opting instead for multi-species romance beneath an orange moon was quickly lampooned and vilified. Far from being the challenging vision of a bright new future full of hope and potential, Gene Roddenbury (genius behind the concept) hoped, as far as the reviewers were concerned it was simply Gun Smoke in space. Aliens instead of Indians and warp drive instead of wagon trains but basically the same old formula. Travel the galaxy, meet up with the baddies and knock seven kinds of green stuffing out of them. The idea that humankind could be living in peace, harmony and prosperity in only a couple of centuries from now seemed hopelessly far fetched and optimistic in the face of the Vietnam War and McCarthyism. While seeming to hold out the promise of equal rights for all races and colours in the future, Lt. Uhura, the first African American on the bridge was (reviewers maintained) basically a glorified telephonist who seemed to spend most of her time opening a channel and scanning hailing frequencies rather than really getting in on the action.

With this in mind, while true fans are not to be deflected by such mean spirited and unwarranted criticism, the non fan isn't simply someone who doesn't care about Star Trek. They are more likely to actively see it as pointless, ridiculous and hopelessly out of touch with reality - in common with their view of the fans themselves. Star Trek isn't simply either "cool" or "ok". If it isn't cool then it's seen as deeply, deeply sad. In common with quite a lot of other things if you stop to think about it. Star Trek, train spotting, bird watching and collecting stamps are all loved by some but broadly viewed as "sad" by many. Tea in the Park, Converse All Stars, Anything To Do With Mobile Phones and recreational drugs are, on the other hand, all now apparently "cool".

Things can of course slip from one category to the other and back again. Doctor Who, for example, was once very cool, then became sad and now seems to be quite cool again. Top of the Pops used to be about as cool as it's possible to be then became pretty sad before being killed off altogether. This of course makes TOP2 doomed to the depths of sadness until that gets the heave-ho as well, then maybe in 20 years time it'll end up being cool as well. Smoking was once very cool, then went completely out of fashion for the generation suffering the after effects and now seems to be "in" again among a younger generation who as yet still think they'll live forever and hence don't need to worry about the health warnings on the packet. James Bond however has always been cool and always will be. And as for Fair Isle jumpers - sorry, I don't know quite how to break this to you…

Confused? I don't blame you. How on earth are mere middle aged humanoids living on a class M planet and brought up with Kirk, Spock, McCoy and Scotty and thinking them pretty cool supposed to keep up with everything we're now expected to like and despise in the 21st century. Unfortunately, that old chestnut "if you have to ask the price you can't afford it" applies. The essence of sadness and coolness seems to be just knowing and not having to ask. The only code of coolness is that if it's cool and you haven't cottoned on yet that makes you pretty sad. Similarly, if you still like something that's passed from coolness to sadness you are also up the creek.

Doesn't it make you just want to shout "Stop!!! So what if I like diesel multiple units, willow warblers, first day covers and come to that Star Trek. What's the problem??? You, on the other hand may prefer Lost, Online Gaming, Sushi and downloading ring tones. Fair enough…." And in that regard maybe a Star Trek future where people seem to be able to tolerate difference does certainly seem to have something to commend it. Jean-Luc Picard would know what to say. Make it so!

And again and again and again...

Even since the dawn of time there has always been a struggle between innovation and conservatism. Every new invention or development has had its apparent downside and for every winner there have always been those that felt like losers, at least in the short term. Enter the wheel. "Not on your Nelly" say the lifters and carriers. In fact the Hewers of Wood, Carriers of Water and Allied Trades raised a motion at their annual conference to have nothing to do with any flat, round objects attached to axles the use of which might contribute to the conveyance of any of the materials to which they have had long established traditional responsibilities. Eventually however, and after considerable internal debate between the "modernisers" and "traditionalists", the wheel prevailed opening up the way eventually for the Trans-Siberian Express and the E-type Jag. Also sadly the Austin Maestro but the less said about that the better.

Anyway, as the years have gone on we have probably grown both more accepting of change - what else can you do - but also more inclined to worry deep down that it'll probably all end in tears some day. Global warming, childhood obesity and the inexorable rise of Graham Norton seem to bear this out.

However, all is not lost for I have recently discovered the Holy Grail of technological change. That innovation for which there is no discernible downside. Something, believe it or not, which cheers but does not inebriate, which adds pleasure without alloy and which doesn't make you fat, poor, weird or alienated from friends, family, colleagues or the cat. No, it isn't the loyal and trusty MP3 player (good as it is), nor even the projecting alarm clock which can tell you in numbers three feet high how late you are for work. Better than all of these. It's Listen Again from the good old BBC!

Blimey, some you may be saying, what's that? Sounds a bit like trying to hold a conversation with the wife's Auntie Bella. Many more are of course now saying - that old thing, we've been using it for years. Well, whatever camp you fall into, the wonders of Listen Again have only just become apparent in the temple of Loose Talk and by jiminy, it's right good. Basically it's the facility to listen again (hence the clever choice of name) to whatever you missed on the radio during the week. In fact not just during the week, but to some extent during the year, decade or even lifetime. So as well as the What's On Diary from yesterday morning and all the boring political drivel poured out by "serious" news radio, you can also get Hancock's Half Hour from 1959, Steptoe and Son from 1963, I'm Sorry I Haven't a Clue from 1972 (sounds exactly the same as last week's edition) and Dad's Army from any time over the past 150 years.

It's great. It's like getting a second chance to chortle, wheeze and bellow with laughter at things you missed, didn't know existed, wouldn't have understood if you did, weren't allowed to listen to or simply hadn't grasped the magic of the first time around. What a fantastic facility. Now they've done it with radio of course I'm desperate for those that serve us up our bill of fare to apply the principle in other areas that would equally benefit. The scope is enormous and limited only by your imagination. In other words, now we've got Listen Again, I'm waiting for Live It Again. Just imagine…

Personally, I'd like to start with birthdays and Christmases. The Scalextric set I got in 1968 at the age of 10 which led to many happy hours with pals re-enacting Le Mans, the Indianapolis 500 and the chase scene from last night's James Bond film. The pleasure that gave on the day and for years to come could certainly stand to be experienced a few times more. Then maybe a couple of (highly selected) holidays, particularly including the all expense paid couple of days in a posh health spa hotel won by the wife in a woman's magazine competition. I'm even willing to put up with the photographer and PR intrusion. All working as it ought to, of course, I could just turn off at that bit and have all the pleasure and none of the pain. Which perhaps might lead on to the subject of girlfriends. Or perhaps not…

Anyway, I would then be looking to regularly rewind Great Concerts I Have Been To, particularly the Pink Floyd tribute band I took our youngest to see in Aberdeen earlier this year. Magic. Parties would be good too. The 60s theme night rave up we had with some friends (some of whom were even recognisable) would be well up there, along with our recent silver wedding do. Anyway the list could go on and on.

Maybe - like MySpace and YouTube - there could even be scope for having other people's top experiences on line to enjoy and you could share your own. Whoa - perhaps on second thoughts that's getting a bit too weird!

Unfortunately, coming back to reality, it may be some time before even BBC technology allows this sort of thing. Tony Hancock and the Goons may be do-able, all the best bits of life (as we know it) are probably never going to be reliveable- except as we remember them. Once they're gone they're gone and we have to go on to the next one. So maybe, that being the case, we just have to make sure there are as many good ones as we can fit it and they are as much fun and benefit for us, our circle of friends and maybe even that tiny chunk of total strangerdom we can influence for good as possible. Seize the Day as the Romans used to say (in Latin of course), or as one former colleague put it "Nobody on their death bed says 'I wish I'd spent more time at the office'".

So if that's the case, what better than to start the process with Christmas this year. Make it a good one. Enjoy yourself, and take pleasure in the wide variety of flavours served up in the mix of friends, family and loved ones you have around you (not literally please). Do some good for someone else in a completely random and unplanned way. Make up your mind to find out what it's all about underneath the razzamatazz, hypocrisy and commercialism. What exactly was going in the manger in the stable that has changed all of human history.

Then you'll have memories to keep you smiling and laughing out loud throughout the rest of the year - in between episodes of Hancock's Half Hour of course.

Countdown to the Perfect Christmas

...well maybe

Christmas. Don't you just love it. Or hate it. The one thing not many of us feel about Christmas is neutral. It's actually quite hard to imagine someone saying. "Oh yeah. Christmas. It's ok I suppose - I can take it or leave it" and really meaning it. If you don't bother about Christmas then it's an active sort of not bothering. If you do bother then the bothering is more frantic rather than merely just "active".

Personally I do love it. Except for the bits I just can't stand. I do love (in no particular order) the first flakes of snow - especially on Christmas morning as we've had a couple of times in the past few years; the grub; the family get-togethers; the sense of anticipation; chestnuts roasting by an open fire (so long as they're not my chestnuts); pressies (of course); Carol services; The Snowman on TV; having friends and neighbours round and most of all everything summed up in the simple phrase "God with us".

The thing I hate most is "perfect Christmas" propaganda. You know the sort of thing, particularly in Women's magazines and particularly many of the better quality ones: "In this issue, the Good Homekeeping countdown to a perfect Christmas. All you need to know to make it perfect on the day..." Very few days in life are perfect and in my experience that mostly happens entirely by accident. In some fantastic, unplanned way things work out better than you thought possible. You make a new friend in a totally unexpected way. A bit of romance blossoms where you least expected it. You hear some distant music and walk round the corner to hear a complete genius busking in a doorway. Whatever you might think would make a perfect day, the one thing is, you can't bottle it and dish it up to order.

Perfect Christmas propaganda tells you that whatever the rest of your life is like, Christmas Day can still be everything it's meant to be. You may have debt up to and beyond your ears, relationships may be on the rocks (wife, husband, partner, kids, colleagues - take your pick), your career may be going down the pan, your landlord may be about to chuck you out, you may have failed/ be failing/likely to fail all your exams, you may even be in the clink waiting for time off for good behaviour. But never fear, for one day in the year things can be "perfect" by the simple expedient of getting the sprouts on in time and having enough light and fluffy mince pies and brandy butter to go round.

As if life wasn't hard enough for lots of folks without this unrealistic and completely unnecessary pressure. Life is life. If things are going well then Christmas can be great fun. If everything else is up the creek then it's hard to see how reality can be persuaded to take a hike, leaving you with a tiny island of perfection in place of all the muddle, frazzle and trauma going on the other 364 days. I suppose it might owe something to that famous story of Christmas in the trenches during the First World War when British and German troops laid down their arms and played football on Christmas Day - only to resume the carnage the day after. Unfortunately even Christmas often isn't enough to stop domestic carnage as the kids squabble, the grown ups grump and everyone feels guilty because this day of all days everyone is supposed to be "nice".

So what's to be done? In a weird sort of way there may be something in the countdown principle but not as it's commonly portrayed. For example instead of:

1st Oct: bake Christmas cake (recipe on p 34.) and put to store
1st Nov: order cards from charity catalogue (see our separate feature
   on where your Christmas card money can do most good)
1st Dec: place your fresh turkey order (how about capon or goose?)

Why not try

1st Oct: make up your mind not to overspend this year and stick to it whatever the kids claim "all" their friends are getting for Christmas
1st Nov: mend fences with the neighbours you don't get on with and invite them to your fireworks party so you can at least be talking to them over Christmas
1st Dec: do something unexpectedly generous for someone you're close to that's got nothing at all to do with Christmas, Ramadan, Diwali or any other celebration - just cause it feels good - for both of you.
I suppose it's all a question of focus. Of course there's nothing wrong with a sensible schedule for cooking Christmas dinner, in fact it may be really helpful and get you through the day without resorting to violence, blasphemy or the cooking sherry. But frankly, most of us have a few more

fundamental things to deal with that will actually have a lot more impact in the long run. Sensible living goes on all year round and when we get the big picture sorted, 25th December can be great, but so can March 13th, August 4th and October 29th. As you know.

Of course, just while we're on the big picture, it might also be worth considering - what's it all about anyway??? We are all aware that fewer and fewer people in the UK have the faintest idea what all the fuss is actually for, what we are, at least nominally, supposed to be celebrating, and whether any of it is of more than merely historical interest. Here's something my wife Fiona wrote some time ago that puts it better than anything I've heard for years, and brings an unexpected touch of class to the corridors of Loose Talk…

Thoo'll hiv tae yeus the byre beuy
For the hoose is burstan fill
This census is that busy min
Wae the bairns aall aff the skeul

Wur aa' been ap fae crack o dawn
And deun waark as wur eeble
Wur stripped and dighted aa' the rooms
But wur never touched the steeble

I'd like tae gae thee more beuy
But tak thoo whit I hae
I can see thoo're fairly puggled
And thee donkey's needan strae

I see thee wife is lippnan'
The bairn's weel on the wey
So tak this sek and bed her doon
Shae'll deu fine on the hey.

Me byre's cheust a byre
Me bes' are aal cheust kye
But I ken this bairn is different
See! merry dancers in the sky.

Choices, choices everywhere -

and not a pause to think…

Here's a scene that strikes fear into the heart of almost any man. You're about to go out on the town with your nearest and dearest. You, as custom dictates, are wearing your second best suit, or jacket and trousers, or maybe even smart but casual jeans and a black shirt. In any case the choices aren't too difficult since nothing you wear is going to make that much difference to your waistline, hairline or jaw line, i.e. you're rather stuck with what you've got and dressing it up can only make a marginal improvement.

Your spouse however has a different perspective. Despite the fact you think she looks terrific in whatever she might choose to wear, from her point of view the choice of costume is crucial. She doesn't want to overdress and look posh or underdress and look as if she can't be bothered. She needs to have everything "matching" (still a mysterious concept to many men) but also wants to take advantage of that fantastic bargain she got in last month's sale. Then there's that almost unworn pair of velvet trousers she got from her sister who can't get into them after Christmas that would look good with the jacket from Debenhams and the shoes she bought with birthday money from Auntie Brenda. And that's even before we consider hair up, hair down, make up (lots, some or none at all) or anything to do with earrings, necklace, brooches, scarves and bags. It's a tough life. No wonder many men are champing at the bit and glancing at their watch every 30 seconds while their women are still only inching towards a decision and may appear somewhat lacking in a sense of urgency - only from the male point of view of course…

Now however, just when you thought we were getting somewhere, the real problem lurches into sight. There's a cry from upstairs, "Would you come up here a minute and tell me what you think?" Uh-oh. There's no getting out of it now. You have to give an opinion. Not only that but it's an opinion that may be questioned and have to be justified. So not just "The pink one looks nice" and there's an end to it. What happens when she pauses for a second then murmurs disarmingly "Not the black one then?" Simply resorting to "Well, the black one would be good too" isn't

44

going to work. That's tantamount to saying "Frankly my dear, I don't give a hoot. As long as we can leave this side of 11.30 p.m. and not be the last ones there I'll be happy." No, you have to sound thoughtful and considered. Desperately you're groping for some reason why the pink one takes the biscuit and the black gets less favoured status. Maybe lots of other people might be wearing black. That might be in favour of the pink as there's less chance of turning up in the same dress as someone else - often deemed to be a problem. On the other hand maybe we wouldn't want to stand out and give the wrong impression. What to do? Trinny and Susannah - help!

Although not frankly the life of man (or women) and a situation any middle aged husband or partner worth his salt really ought to be able to navigate with ease, this often played out little scenario does highlight a problem that turns up elsewhere too. There seems to be an assumption all over the place that more choices would be better and fewer choices would be worse. Education is a prime example. The idea of empowering parents to be able to choose which school their offspring attends is thought to be "a good thing". Being stuck with the one size fits all local establishment is deemed "not good enough". Frankly, however, like the hapless husband on a couples night out, many of us simply aren't equipped to make a sensible choice. How can we tell whether school A's excellence in literacy and numeracy should be more highly rated than school B's good reputation for a positive ethos, excellence in arts and music and good playing fields. Would it be too simplistic to suggest that what most parents want is a great all round education at the local school without having to invoke a choice to go elsewhere - something I think we are generally pretty blessed with locally. And that could apply across the board to lots of other stuff like health, social care, policing, street cleaning or whatever you like. The choice we want is for things to be pretty good where we are without having to shop around.

Our dilemmas as partners and parents pale into insignificance however next to the really big choices faced by our young people. In an age of increasing choice the range of options now available must seem frankly bewildering to many of them. Courses, colleges and careers there are aplenty with pros and cons for each. The trick seems to be not only amassing all the information and weighing up alternatives but then being able to understand the personalities and aptitudes concerned and get the right fit for the right person. Square pegs and at least sort of square-ish holes if possible.

Another factor a bit different today is the reality that most of the current generation will probably have multiple careers over their working lives. Far from the quiz master of life saying "I'm sorry, I'll have to accept your first answer," they are more likely to be told "Yes, that's interesting. Are you sure you'd like to stick with that. There's plenty of time. Maybe you want to move on to something else and come back to that one later…" At my fortieth birthday, around the time I was planning a career move, the birthday card that struck most of a chord showed a short, fat, bandy bloke in a tutu looking thoroughly out of place among the swan lake chorus line. The text said, "Being a grown up means not having to stick with your first choice…"

In one area however young people face choices in 2006 that might not be so different from 1906 or even 1066. Part of growing up concerns making choices about character - ultimately a great deal more important than mere careers. It's about who you choose to be, whose example you follow and what values and attitudes you adopt. Like slightly bewildered travellers trying to find the right platform and board the right train, young folk are daily assailed by life's customer service announcements, information broadcasts and travel bulletins right, left and centre. The problem of how to help our young people get towards the sort of adult life both they and we can be proud of makes the poser "Does my bum look big in this" not seem so taxing after all. And like career choices which may wobble a bit before moving off in hopefully the right direction, we as parents need to exercise a bit of understanding and patience as character forms.

Looking on the bright side however, at least it doesn't involve saying what dress matches what skirt, shoes, bag and lipstick and whether we'd prefer the pink, black, navy, tartan or tangerine. What a relief - there might be some hope after all.

Go on - change one thing - or maybe even two!

Have you noticed the Change One Thing campaign on the go just now? Little leaflets and fliers are to be found lying about in the chemists, doctors surgeries, health promotion and so on. While waiting in the queue to pay for my monthly supply of anti-balding miracle cure, assorted slimming aids and herbal mood enhancers (thank goodness the nappy buying days are over), the slogan caught my eye and set me thinking. What one thing would I change for 2007 and - on the other hand - what things do I want to remain exactly as they are?

Of course, in explaining the Change One Thing approach, the leaflet goes on to point out that in thinking about changes you might want to make you've got to be specific, realistic, achievable and so forth. All very sensible I dare say, but within the confines of this column, I think we can let our imaginations run a bit free-er and happily include the vague and general, unrealistic and probably never achievable at least in this life. Well you've got to dream a bit haven't you.

The first question of course is who do we want to change? The campaign is clearly aimed at changing things about yourself but, let's face it, many of our lives would be greatly enhanced by some major changes in the life, demeanour and habits of those with whom we have the pleasure of sharing the planet. First off there's that annoying whistler you have to share an office with. The last thing you need with deadlines looming and the pressure mounting is the Roger Whittaker interpretation of Abba's greatest hits. Whether this change is to be effected by psychological warfare, bad language or super glue is beyond the remit of this column but do let us all know how you get on … Ranging further afield we would of course cut a swathe through Radio One DJs, Celebrity Big Brother contestants, treacherous weather forecasters and drivers who seem to think that indicating is a sign of weakness and prefer to keep you guessing.

But, all the while we realise that this is quite against the spirit of Change One Thing. It's YOU, you're meant to be changing, not other people who have the misfortune not to fit in with your view of the world, musical taste or driving habits. Yes, I know, not nearly so much fun but still - it has to be done. But what to change? So many imperfections, so little motivation… The Change One Thing leaflet, again choosing to err on the side of sane and sensible changes mentions such worthy topics as "Giving up Smoking", "Losing some weight", "Taking More Exercise" and so on. No big surprises there then. If you'd like somewhat more personalised suggestions I'm sure your nearest and dearest might oblige. Like - "For goodness sake lose the maroon jumpers" or "Will you take your muddy boots off before tramping right through the living room!" Even "It might be nice if somebody other than me thought about emptying the bins now and again" How coarse, narrow-minded and commonplace you might think and you might be right - but maybe they're also entitled to a few changes for the better. Sad but probably true.

Anyway, this is again perhaps missing the point. This is supposed to be about life enhancing changes. Things that will help you to actualise your inner potential, free the spirit and counter negative vibrations - not just keep the carpet a wee bit cleaner and better manage your domestic waste. So yet again - what are we to change? Well frankly, only you can say. The only wrong answer is "I have no idea - beats me." The point is that life with all its practicality does have a sickening tendency to take the dreams, visions and ambitions all of us have from time to time and slowly but surely squeeze the life out of them. The feeling that you need to extend your social circle a bit and make some new friends, your ambition to learn to paint or play the harmonium, your lifelong desire to canoe through the foothills of the Pyrenees or your hope to somehow escape your humdrum job and open a craft shop - all might be possible, you never know. The fact is that there are people who have done all of these things - that's to say, some people have done each of them - probably not the same person doing all of them…

The point is that when you were young you thought life would go on forever. People die, yes, but only other people. Somewhere around your thirties or forties the truth slowly dawns that there comes a time when things you want to do but haven't yet got round to are going to get harder not easier. When you were young you had time and energy but no money. Now you may still be able to summon the energy but find you've neither time nor money. Sometime soon you might find you are completely out of time, money, energy and can't even remember what you needed them for. Clearly now's the time to act. A character in Captain Correlli's Mandolin decides to get married and talks it over with her father. She says:

> "Don't you approve of him, Papakis?"
> He turned and looked at her gently. "He's too young. Everyone is too young when they marry."

Anything we decide to do that's a bit out of the ordinary takes a certain leap of courage and may leave us feeling under prepared and unready for the challenge. Clearly the outcomes will not be known in advance. Nevertheless, nothing ventured…

And finally, as a useful counter to all this shifting sand of change and self-actualisation, it's also maybe worthwhile sparing a thought for things in life we don't want to change. Treasured friendships built up over many years, ways we've been able to help or encourage people we come into contact with, the bedrock of values and norms we - and our families - have come to depend on, even daily routines that give us the sense of stability and community most of us need to provide a context for living.

So, all in all, Change One Thing seems to be not a bad aim for any new year. You could of course throw caution entirely to the winds and change two things. Who knows where it might end…

Take me to... the Land of Lost Socks

...Ball Point Pens and Car Keys

Once upon a time the standard reason for not doing all the things that needed done - like putting up shelves, spending more time with your loved ones or papering the back bedroom - was simple even if not very commendable. Basically you couldn't be bothered, kept putting it off, found a more enjoyable alternative (like being slumped in front of the telly or having a nap) or just downright refused. Time wasn't the problem - it was motivation that was sadly lacking.

Nowadays however things are different. Working late, private study, doing your tax returns, running the kids to everything from Archery to Zen Buddhism for Beginners, essential housework that has to be done in the evening now everybody works all day - all of it is crowding in and squeezing out the important but maybe a bit less urgent side of life. Where on earth am I going to find the time for pressing wild flowers, bottling fruit, learning the mandolin or simply hanging out down the boozer - all of which I was led to believe would be available to modern humans once robots were humming away in the background uncomplainingly doing all the work. Instead we find that robots only appear in adverts (does it qualify them for an equity card, I wonder), the workload keeps on getting ratcheted up and there simply ain't the time to do it all and find that new age nirvana - "quality time for me"!

Now perhaps putting up shelves hasn't always been your number one recreational pursuit. On the other hand, next to being stuck in the office till the stars come out or keeping Adam Hart-Davies happy in the tax department, it maybe seems almost like a therapeutic alternative. The problem is that nowadays we haven't the time even for the necessary evils far less fun time off.

That being the case, new and ingenious ways must be found for making more time and "leveraging" more value out of the time you've got. And there are of course various ways of doing this. Firstly, you can just do all the things you're doing already but do them quicker. Like watching Eastenders in the new high speed edition (only available on cable so far) which plays the standard episodes but at 1½ times the speed. The characters all run around like headless chickens and talk in gibberish. So not much change there then. But at least you get to be confused and breathless sitting down. Try applying the 1½ speed approach to mowing the lawn or digging the garden. Don't even think about washing the dog!

Alternatively, to lapse into management-speak, "don't work harder, work smarter". In practical terms this is equivalent to not just pressing down a bit more on the accelerator but trying to find a short cut home. So you might consider telling Mr. Brown that you actually didn't earn anything last year having weighed up the benefit of all the time you'll save (probably in the teens of hours) versus the probability of further demands latter on (up to and including time spent behind bars). So maybe that's not such a good choice. Or you might decide to collapse your keep fit regime and housework. Jogging while doing the ironing may take a little practice but I'm sure you could get the hang of it…

Next up is the no-brainer - pay somebody else to do the stuff you hate that's devouring all your valuable leisure time. House cleaning is certainly option number one here and is not uncommon. Garden chores also sometimes qualify and the principle might even apply to shopping, cooking the tea or what is now euphemistically called valeting your car (it used to just be hoovering when I had to grumpily do it for my Dad). All fine and well, but to really make inroads you'll have to be a lot more radical than that. Think how much more time you'd have if you didn't fritter it all away browsing the wonderful Internet. Answer - pay someone else to waste their time (with a full written report delivered weekly) and instead do something you enjoy that actually makes sense. Or if you're going to take things to extremes, you might even employ a professional to bicker with your partner which leaves you free to enjoy the game of golf you were going to be fighting about. Of course, they might be employing a surrogate bicker-er too which could lead to unexpected consequences if they both decide to settle on terms neither of you would consider for a moment. Also kids who apply this principle to homework often come unstuck for what now seem like petty and old fashioned reasons.

Finally, my last and best suggestion is to ruthlessly hunt out pointless activity and banish it into outer darkness. And number one in the pointless activity stakes has to be hunting for things you've lost. I know I don't need to elaborate, but let me anyway… socks, keys, wallets, documents, glasses, bills, cheque book, credit cards, potato peeler ("Who can live without it I ask in all honesty…"), newspapers, a full set of table mats, sunglasses, spare coat hangers, mobile phones, passports (bad one that), plectrums (if you have a guitarist in the house), gloves, razor, swimming trunks, maps, wellies, the bag of fertiliser you could swear you bought last year, your special birthday mug, remote controllers (six or eight at the last count), batteries, light bulbs, pens, pencils, rubbers, rulers, calculators, holiday brochures - need I go on. You've lost them, I've lost them, all God's children done lost them. And the time you spend looking for them would guarantee you at least half a lifetime more - not to mention the beneficial effects of easing the additional stress of looking for things you need now, instantly, immediately, right this second! It would drive you to drink if you could find the bottle opener.

What's to be done about it then? Saying "just stop losing things" is a counsel of perfection and hence pointless. You could follow option 1 (above) and just look quicker, option 2 and only look for things of high value and ignore the rest which might eventually involve eating potatoes still coated in muck off the floor while wearing only one sock in an unshaved condition (you - not the sock), or option 3 and pay someone else to look for them, which might work but in our case would mean permanently adding an extra member to the household which might have a bit of a downside in itself.

Happily however I think I've come up with a solution - easy, elegant, cheap and effective. Simply re-designate the activity of looking for lost things as a hobby which you enjoy, value and look forward to. There you are. Problem solved. Ta-daa!

When Two Tribes go to War...

..make mine a lentil soup

A nineteenth century Duke of Argyll once remarked that there are two kinds of people in the world – those who are good to their servants and those who aren't. Notwithstanding that the servants might have a view, this does highlight something that seems intriguing about opinion and points of view both then and now, namely, the temptation to see the world in 2D. Everything comes down to two alternatives. Us and them. People like me and the rest. Good guys and bad guys. Truth and justice or the evildoers. The ways of the force and the dark side. Or less apocalyptically, tea or coffee, Coke or Pepsi, PC or Mac, and Beatles or Stones (more recently Blur or Oasis). Whether Rangers and Celtic count as a matter of life and death or are actually more important than that, I'll leave you to decide.

Whatever the issue however, there is something very comforting about believing yourself to be in the majority shareholding with everything sussed out - living "in the light". It reminds me of a prayer I once heard for "the electricians who sit in darkness" which left you wondering about their electrical expertise as well as the state of their souls. If you are in the light, that leaves others in darkness with not much in between. However, even if in every particular case it turns out that your own view happens to be right as defined by the Royal Society, the General Assembly, MORI and even the Magic Circle, one or two problems still arise.

Firstly, this world is just too glorious and varied a place for only two opinions to be worth choosing from on most subjects. It's like being asked your favourite colour. How can you possibly choose between the dappled greens of a woodland walk, a band of flaming crimson sky at sunset, dazzling reflections off a bank of snow or the chocolate textures of a ploughed field. Or maybe it's even worse. Like asking whether you prefer cream of tomato soup or Chick Murray. It makes no sense to put it like that and the world would be immensely poorer without either. (c.f. Chick's joke about when he'd had a skinful and ended up on his backside at a bus stop. "What are you doing down there?" asks a scandalised shopper. "Have you had too much to drink?" "No," says

Chick. "I'm just trying to break a bar of chocolate in my back pocket.") Secondly, once established in any single opinion, it can get harder and harder to see any good in the other side. Challenges to the established view tend to put us all behind the barricades rather than coming out – even gingerly at first – to see if there's something worth looking a bit more closely at. That's what makes it impossible for the Shadow Chancellor to admit that Gordon Brown has actually done a pretty fair job on the economy, or for Tony to come clean and say what we all know (or at least hope) he feels in private – that the war has been an enormous gamble embarked upon for wholly spurious reasons. Admitting that the other team has some good players or the other band some good tunes makes you look like a bit of a wuss. Like you're breaking the rules of debate and not only won't be taken seriously by the other side but even yourself feel slightly wishy-washy.

We have a wee plaque in the kitchen that gives the meaning of my wife's name. "From the Gaelic meaning 'fair'. She is a good listener who will weigh up both sides of an argument. She has strong values in life." We don't have a "Les" one but if it exists, I imagine it would say "Les, named after a small town in Fife. Makes up his mind without considering all or sometimes even any of the evidence. Once decided he is impossible to shift, regardless of relevant facts. Do not allow this man anywhere near an opinion column." Naturally enough Mrs. Cowan's well rounded view of things can be somewhat provoking. It must be said she is much more tolerant of my dogmatism. However like Rick Waller flapping past the gym, I can at least see the benefit even if I'm not yet fully engaged. And at times of elections and important national debate it does seem reasonably important to consider all the evidence before coming to a decision - not just going for the well worn option.

And if you're wondering where I stand on any of the key agendas, let me be quite clear, it's Irn Bru, the abacus, Falkirk Bairns and lentil soup.

Oh give me a home where no hoodies can roam

Fed up with hooded skateboarders clattering past the front door at 3am leaving a trail of upset rubbish, jeers and taunts in their wake? Irritated by primary kids in the sweet shop taking half an hour to decide they want a 50p mix? Kept awake till the wee small hours by boy racers aiming to set a new Kirkwall Speed Record? Or just beginning to feel your age and in need of a wee bit peace and quiet…

What you need is the latest concept in security, prosperity and peace of mind. A well established concept in the US - particularly Florida, California and Miami - but coming to a location near you very soon. It's safe, secure, peaceful and reserved exclusively for people like you. It's clean, orderly, well designed and tranquil. Not a note of rap music is to be heard for miles around, for here Barry Manilow and the Carpenters reign supreme. What is it? The latest concept in age appropriate living - the Retirement Village.

Some years ago US real estate developers hit on the concept of reorganising the world in favour of those over 60s with a low tolerance of "yooff" and enough spare cash to make sure they never have to come into contact with them again. Hence was born the intriguing concept of what we now call the "retirement village". In essence it's basically a gated community for older residents with housing, services and entertainment all built in - and anyone under 25 strictly built out. Some variations do allow grandchildren to visit on the second Sunday afternoon of alternate months but only if bound, gagged and sedated first and only briefly visible between the car and tradesman's entrance.

Unaccompanied teenagers are absolutely verboten as are car stereos, iPods, music less than 25 years old, the word "Yo!", addressing anyone as "dude" or "ma man", backwards baseball caps, torn jeans, goth gear, and anything the security staff could reasonable describe as energetic. TVs are tuned only to Countdown and Emmerdale, radios to the Archers and Woman's Hour, only the Daily Mail and Daily Express fight for counter space in the Newsagents and the Internet is filtered to only allow access to nature, wildlife and knitting websites.

Well, that's a complete caricature of what over 60s want of course - and a complete caricature of what teenagers are like, but the success of the retirement village concept, and its spread to the UK does suggest that there are people who find the idea of cutting themselves off from nasty disturbing youth quite attractive. What they seem to want is a world without all of the noise, disturbance and disruption they think young people bring with them. Forgetting of course that this also keeps at bay all of the vitality, creativity, freshness and originality young people also bring into the world.

And this isn't only a problem to do with housing. From time to time we hear of new research going on into extending life expectancy - perhaps indefinitely - as genetic research gathers pace and the idea of growing and transplanting new organs developed with your own genetic makeup becomes possible. But hang on a bit. If the world's resources are limited and the older generation just keep getting older without making any more room, what's the implication? Clearly there's going to be less and less space for a new generation to arrive and take its place. Think of it. Maybe no more of whatever social ills we associate with some younger people, but also no more of everything we associate with new life, new thoughts and new ways of seeing the world. It's like saying we like autumn so much and do not look forward to winter so we're going to ban Spring (and eventually Summer as well) and keep everything locked at about the first week in September.

Nobody would argue with the benefit of increasing active, healthy life (of course) but while we're doing that, we've also got to remember that the human race functions by constantly renewing itself - socially, creatively, artistically, morally and we hope spiritually as well. Let's face it, it's the current mid and older generations that have landed this generation of young people with the greatest problems the world has ever faced - and it will be they who have to solve them, not us.

So the next time you have to walk around a gaggle of noisy teenagers on Broad Street, or give the neighbours' kids their ball back (again) or tidy your offspring's bedroom (how many times???) or read another shock / horror exposé into inner city housing estates and ASBOs and start to daydream about your future retirement prospects and a life of peace and quiet, don't forget where everything good in the world has ultimately come from as well as some things we'd be better off without. YOOFF! Cool.

Stand back ladies - this is a man's job

What is it about men and barbecues?
Does anybody really know???

Summer is here and with it the barbecuing season. Picture the scene.
Either:

it's a glorious Saturday afternoon and all's well with the world, or
it's an overcast Tuesday evening and maybe the rain might hold off or
any alternative in between…

Now, somebody foolishly lets the word barbecue drop from their lips or
unsought and unbidden it pops into hubby's otherwise freewheeling brain.
And that moment the damage is done. He's in the garage digging out the
ancient, rusty barbecuing stuff including a moth eaten bag of briquettes
the bottom of which is just about to fall out, and a damp and fusty packet
of firelighters. Then he's in the kitchen scrubbing the grill bit with an old
Brillo pad, remembering to leave deep gouges in the new ceramic sink
and cover every surface with brown soapy sludge. Then he's on his
knees in front of the freezer digging down through aeons of geological
time - i.e. food that was bought the summer before last - in search of
burgers, pork chops, chicken, steak - maybe even mince or frozen
prawns if there's nothing else…

Then - if, against all the odds, he can find everything he needs or some
reasonable substitute - it's into the garden, or garage if it's raining, half
a hundredweight of charcoal and a dozen firelighters dumped into the
trough and a match applied. Sometimes a match and half a gallon of
petrol are applied (not in that order) but by hook or by crook he eventually
gets it going.

Now comes the audience participation element of this happy summer
party game. Wife / partner / helper / weekend visitor are all encouraged
to do the real work of preparing a salad, baked potatoes, dips, buttered
rolls and garlic bread, drinks etc., rousting out cutlery and crockery and
setting the garden furniture back upright. (It may also of course need the
attention of a Brillo pad but there's no time for that now…) Barbecuing
man cannot of course assist in any of these minor ancillary matters

because he is standing over said barbecue en garde with tongs and extra petrol in case it goes out … or stays lit … or just smoulders for half an hour.

Anyway, eventually the time comes for meat to be applied. Generally this is the moment he remembers that he hasn't defrosted it yet. But if he has or has even thought ahead to get fresh stuff (unlikely I grant you), on it goes. Now, as all the gods of barbecuing know, this moment is supposed to be when the charcoal has all gone a uniform grey colour and has stopped smoking. Barbecue man treats this more like a guideline than a definite rule. So it may be 95% ready or even just over 10% ready - in either case "that'll probably do" so on it goes.

At this point there are various options of what might happen next. Alternatively, all food items remain raw on the inside while seared jet black on the outside. Or they may remain raw on the inside while also pretty much raw outside too. One time in a hundred they may actually be edible. Food that no-one would dream of accepting in a restaurant has to be bravely gnawed through while balancing the really edible stuff on a paper plate on your lap only to see it end up on the deck or get slavered over by the dog. As the rain comes on…

By this point anyone with any brains has dumped the variously raw and incinerated health hazard, filled up on crisps and salad and opened another bottle of wine.

So that's roughly it. But why???

Clearly, such eccentric behaviour is likely to be complex and hard to fully understand. However, while I'm waiting for my research grant to come through, a few possible explanations come to mind…

Firstly there's the Neanderthal interpretation. This suggests that since man (and it is overwhelmingly the male of the species) had been hunkering over the cave campfire for countless generations and since modern life has parted us from cave dwellings and (courtesy of the Health and Safety Executive) bonfires, just about the only thing you can legally set fire to these days is charcoal. By this explanation, the food cooked on the barbecue is merely an accessory to the main activity and barbecuing could in fact be done without any major loss of function were there no edible outputs whatsoever. Which is more or less what happens anyway. Secondly, there is the hunter provider explanation. This also involves incantations round the communal fire, but this time as a celebration dance following a successful hunt and kill. Ancient man has seen the herd of mammoths. He has grouped together with others of the tribe. He has sharpened his spear and gone in pursuit of said hairy beasts. Mammoth burgers ("not less than three stone of fresh meat in every one") have been brought back and now must be cooked and provided to the tribe. Now frankly, you have to admit that the weekly trolley derby at the supermarket does lack a certain something in comparison. Hence the need from time to time to re-enact the rituals of the past, set fire to something and COOK!

Finally we have the alternative - and still somewhat controversial - new man explanation. This approach underplays stone age influences and instead tends to emphasise current social roles and practices. New man knows he has to go shopping. He knows he has to be "kitchen friendly". He knows he has to take his fair share of the housework and child care - while also putting up shelves, getting a promotion at work, mowing the lawns and reading to the kids. How can it all be done - or how can it be done successfully when nowadays new woman can basically do everything new man can do but better? Here's the solution. Find some activity new woman is not the least bit interested in, realises is a pointless waste of time (and steak) and basically sees no benefit in. Here's new man's opportunity to move in, make it his own and excel. Hence the ritual of the charcoal and the firelighters.

Now, having devoted considerable time, energy and study to this subject I can see some element of truth in all three perspectives. All have their merits and frankly it's not at all easy to come to a definitive conclusion.

I think more research is required…

I think I need to move to sunnier climes to find out…

I think I need a new barbecue set…

It's Official. Loose Talk is a Pile of Pants

I was interested - and a bit surprised - to hear recently that the Oxford English Dictionary has just included in its periodic update of new words, the term "bahooky". Now as far as I'm concerned bahookies have been around since the dawn of time and have certainly been referred to as such at least since my childhood and probably for many hundreds of years before that. What is a bahooky you ask? Well, if you're not standing up as you're reading this, then your bahooky is what you're sitting on. No, not the new leather recliner next the magazine rack - your bottom! Actually the OED people define it as "dialect, chiefly Scot. buttock"

Now to me "buttocks" has always had something of a medical feel to it (so to speak) as in "the patient showed considerable inflammation of the buttocks due to excessive exposure to ultra violet rays…" i.e. a sunburnt bum from falling asleep in a skimpy bikini on the beach in Marbella. For normal people (sorry to all medics partaking this month), your choice of description of that part of the anatomy to which we all know we're referring depends a fair bit on your upbringing and that ticklish area of what is considered acceptable talk and what is considered rude or taboo. And that varies a lot.

In my childhood the good old Anglo Saxon "arse", despite having been on the go for over 800 years (look it up in Chaucer if you don't believe me), was absolutely verboten and any mention of the word would receive a swift and stinging slap thereon by way of correction. Maybe I grew up in far too delicate surroundings but even "bum" was a bit beyond the pale in our household so we had to make do with the inoffensive but rather lacking in character "bottom". Bottom didn't seem to carry the force of meaning you sometimes needed though so we had some acceptable alternatives. "Beam end" was ok as in "Just you sit on your beam end and pipe down". Also possible was "tail end" though this could be confusing since shirts also had tail ends and so I suppose had anything else with a tail. Stronger than these was "backside" as in "If I see you do that one more time I'll take my hand off your backside!" Bahooky wasn't rude but it was a bit of a comedy word. Proper usage might include "Did you see Mrs. MacGregor skite on the ice? She fell right on her bahooky!" The totally neutral "behind" was of course also available if nothing else would do. Speaking of which, did you hear about the careless butcher that backed into the bacon slicer and got a wee bit behind in his orders…

Other families, of course, had different standards so imagine my horror through my younger years to hear routine references to bums, arses and more recently butts (thanks Bart) without a whiff of embarrassment. Now courtesy of the Renault ad "shaking that ass" is also apparently acceptable. And more recently still, loosely related to bums and butts, (how loosely you can decide for yourselves) is the wonderful "pile of pants" for everything low down, unattractive and unacceptable.

And that's kind of the point isn't it. Language is constantly changing and a word that may have been ok in one era can become totally unacceptable in another. "N*gg*r" is a good modern example. It has now become so offensive that I can't even spell it out in full for fear of giving offence - and I understand exactly why and agree with the reasons we no longer use it. "Bum" on the other hand is mild to the point of having lost its taboo overtones altogether.

So the question becomes not so much about which specific words we use and more about giving and receiving offence. That makes me think of Max Ehrmann's poem, Desiderata which says:

> Speak your truth quietly and clearly;
> and listen to others,
> even the dull and the ignorant;
> they too have their story.

On the one hand we might say words are just combinations of sounds - what's the big deal? But we all know that what we say can make an enormous difference to the people we say it to. It's all very well to have a laugh at a fantastic insult, like the time Bessie Braddock told Churchill, "Winston, you are drunk, very drunk." To which the great man replied, "Yes. And you are ugly, horribly ugly. But in the morning I shall be sober!" On the other hand we can probably all think of times we've been on the receiving end of some cutting remark which knocked us out for the entire day. Or other times we've been the perpetrators - even if we immediately wanted the earth to swallow us up. What we say, once said, is unfortunately not recyclable - which can be a real bummer! You might think that words are such a liability we should all stick to sign language but you know where that might lead…

So what's to be done about it? Think before you speak is a pretty good motto. You've maybe also heard it said you have two ears and one mouth for a reason - and it's not to fit the headphones that came with your iPod. We also need to be able to not take too seriously offhand remarks we know weren't really intended the way they came out. And that's not even beginning to think about what we now all know as political correctness. (Have you ever been shopping for a new computer in PC World - you've really got to watch what you say in there.)

So Loose Talk's advice this week is don't be a butthead and make sure what you say doesn't come out a pile of pants!

Ye canna change the laws o' physics

- or the laws of queuing

Have you noticed a plethora of geeky science stuff in the media recently? TV, radio and the bookshops all seem to be stuffed with popular science explaining the atom, relativity, quantum this, that and the other, the big bang, the nature of time, string theory, black holes, chaos and parallel dimensions. Now, as far as most of us are concerned, string theory is about why it always ends up in a fankle however well you wind it up and parallel dimensions are when you and your significant other arrange to meet outside the chemist's at quarter to one but sadly choose different chemists. This inevitably leads to chaos as your lunch date disappears into a black hole and you run the risk of a big bang - on the nose. What a good thing you are both so gracious and forgiving. Relatively speaking…

Now, while all of this focuses fascinatingly on the laws of nature - what they are, how they are and sometimes even why they are - what interests me is that other set of laws we've probably all come across, the best known of which is named after the unfortunate Murphy. Simply stated, Murphy's law (also known as Sod's law), claims that if it can go wrong it will - in the worst possible way and at the worst time. So, for example, the day you put your suit into the dry cleaners with the car keys in the pocket happens to be the very day your wife loses hers and needs the spare set. Or the lawnmower runs out of petrol five minutes after the petrol station closes. Or the one time you forget to take the road map is the one time you take a wrong turning, get hopelessly lost and need it. This is also known more informally as jammy side down, which I'm sure needs no further explanation!

So all-convincing and useful have these phenomena become that many have ended up being described as laws - just like the physical set. Hence, in exactly the same way as we have the law of gravity ("what goes up must come down" - except for mortgage payments and petrol prices) we also get the law of queuing. This states that whichever queue you happen to be in, the other one goes quicker. Changing queues does absolutely no good of course because the queue you just left has now become the "other" one and hence goes faster. Now I know you're wondering what would happen if two people simultaneously swap queues - which one would go faster then - but in the only experiment so far conducted as soon as the swap had taken place the fire alarm went off, everyone had to leave the store and when the building was deemed safe again all queues were reset to their original positions. At that point those involved in the experiment decided it might be quicker to remain where they were or else they would never be able to pay for their messages and get home for the tea.

Next up is the famous Parkinson's law. Parkinson is credited with identifying the process whereby work expands to fill available time. So if you have 40 minutes to rattle up a quick macaroni cheese because you're all going out to the pictures and everybody hates missing the start - that's how long it takes. If, on the other hand, you have a day and a half to prepare something really special for your loved one who may be evaluating your kitchen skills as part of the mating process, that is also exactly how long it takes. Even if it is just macaroni cheese. My own humble contribution to Parkinson's Law (the Cowan variation) is to state that work expands to fill available space referring to physical dimensions as well as time. So if you have a tiny kitchen and only three feet of usable worktop space, that gets completely covered with dirty dishes. The same applies to your next house that has double the space and to the next one again that has more worktop than the forestry commission has woodland. And so forth. This is why, guys, your work bench in the garage is always feet deep in tools, off cuts of wood, empty cardboard boxes, spare ceramic tiles and leaky hose while your neighbour's Black and Decker workmate which is only three feet long is in a similar condition. Regardless of how much you potter in the garage, neither of you has any spare capacity - ever.

Similar to that is Hofstadter's Law (no really - it does exist - look it up in Wikipedia). This states that it always takes longer than you expect, even when you take into account Hofstadter's Law. So leave five minutes to pack for your summer holidays and it takes eight. Leave five days and it takes eight days. One subtle effect of the law is that even if you take the tendency to underestimate into account and leave some extra time - it still takes longer. This of course applies to all sorts of activities. One specific variant of Hofstadter's Law is called the Student Syndrome and relates to how long it takes to complete assignments. However long students have, they will always do 98% of the work in the last 2% of the time they have. So give them 6 days and they are rushing and panicking the night before. Give them six months and … they are rushing and panicking the night before. Sound familiar?

Now you could see this as annoying but basically nobody's fault but that of said students. On the other hand the better known Peter Principle causes genuine heartache. That's the one that states that managers inevitably get promoted beyond their level of competence. It works like this. Bob (all names have been changed to protect the guilty) is a brilliant teacher / carer / accountant or cleaner. He is efficient, diligent, cheerful and pays attention to detail. Management eventually notices this and thinks - ah ha - wouldn't he make a great supervisor of teaching, caring, accounting or cleaning. It's more money and bit more responsibility so Bob goes with it - he may even have thought it himself and applied for the job. If he's good at that he's likely to become the supervisor of other supervisors and if he's good at that becomes head honcho. Will he be good at that? Maybe, but the Peter Principle states that the only thing that will definitely stop the process is Bob eventually being useless at whatever he has just been promoted to. How many managers have eventually got beyond the level at which they were any good, or perhaps for easy counting, how many haven't? Frightening isn't it.

So while I'm all for particle accelerators longer than the M25 to smash up atoms and electrons and see what comes out, and telescopes that can look back in time to before there were any Harry Potter books published, I do feel we need more research into things that maybe matter more to most of us. In particular when's my tea going to be ready and will I ever see my power screwdriver again. A management consultant might be helpful to explore these complex problems but you know why I don't want one of those.

Supersize me - and me breeks

Keats called it the season of mists and mellow fruitfulness, close bosom-friend of the maturing sun. Poor Mole fell foul of it by venturing into the Wild Wood to make the acquaintance of Mr. Badger and was then caught out by a sudden snowfall and hoards of malevolent stoats and weasels. In Orkney we call it the back end - which is perhaps more relevant than you might think for reasons that will become apparent. Wikipedia, the online encyclopaedia, says its personifications are usually pretty, well-fed females adorned with fruits, vegetables and seasonal grains. Uppermost in my mind is the fear of it resulting in a far too well fed male adorned with a couple of stone more than was there when I last looked in the Spring.

Autumn - which is what all of the above refer to - comes at the end of a period of extended munching with long hot summer days out picnicking whenever the rain eases up long enough and evening barbecues, inside the garage if need be, followed by holidays in some far flung place where eating and drinking to excess is essential for the genuine Brits abroad experience. End result - none of my breeks fit, getting in and out of the car is beginning to prove a challenge and rather than hunching over a hot computer, nowadays it's more of a sprawl. Let's face it, it's not just the birds that are going south!

And worse is yet to come. After this brief period of almost normal intake, before long we're into the lead up to Christmas and we all know what that means. Starting with the office party, then having the neighbours round, then Granny and Grandpa, then the Church / Club / Society / Anarchist Cell festive nosh up, it's one long assault on our hard pressed innards as if they've had it too good for too long, got careless and now need to be roundly abused until they learn that life is neither kind nor fair.

So this couple of months of autumn proper is, if I can put it this way, at least potentially like a low fat cold meat filling in the white-bread-with-lashings-of-butter sandwich that lies on either side. In other words, your last chance to lose a couple of pounds before festive gluttony gives you the unwelcome opportunity to act as Santa's body double if the old gentleman happens to be much delayed along the way. In a word - not good and your last chance!

Ok - so you've got the resolve but what's to be actually done about it? Should it be low fat, high fibre, low carb, high protein, cabbage soup, fruit and nuts, fish and fowl, sparkling water and bananas or all and every one at the same time? And what of exercise? Should it be a 10 for 9 saver card at the gym, power walking as far as the pub and back regularly every evening, steps, squats, jerks, burpees (whatever they are), 40 lengths every lunchtime or football with the kids? Alternatively you could simply order a broad selection of diet books from Amazon, send for one of these trendy exercise balls the size of a space hopper, put a decision off until they arrive and hope they all get lost in the post. Ultimately not what we're looking for but at least it does do something to ease the guilt and keeps the economy ticking over. In fact, diet authors, the Complan corporation and manufacturers of rowing machines have probably benefited more from general public guilt than Live Aid, makers of Greetings Cards and florists combined.

Actually, if you are feeling guilty about that extra couple of pounds, few inches more, and complete replacement wardrobe, Loose Talk wants to remind you that - as I recently discovered - it turns out that it's actually not your fault. There was a time when constantly stuffing your face with too many chips, burgers, and bangers and mash then ramming the whole lot home with double chocolate chip ice cream and maple syrup simply meant you were a greedy pig and ought to eat less. Now however it turns out to be a simple problem of "portion control". In fact you're probably suffering from portion control misalignment syndrome which can only be treated by hypnotherapy, combined with a cognitive behavioural approach, aversion therapy and possibly minor surgery.

On the other hand if that doesn't take your fancy, you could always follow the Loose Talk Autumn Alternative Last Chance approach.

- Step one - remember what you looked like in the Spring
- Step two - think what you might look like after Christmas
- Step three - EAT A BIT LESS FOR GOODNESS SAKE!

Anyway, that's what I'll be doing. Anybody interested in a hundredweight of unused diet books and the Jane Fonda fitness DVD?

To whom it may concern – Happy Christmas

Ok folks. Goggles on, adjust your snorkel, deep breath then down we go - into another Christmas! TV is full of it, magazines are full of it and the shops of course are full of it. Not to be outdone, this column is also full of it. You may take the view that we've been full of it years now but, on this occasion, Christmas stuff is what we're talking about...

Now, I know the common rant is that Christmas is rubbish and not at all like it used to be. Well, of course that's bound to be the case because back then you were getting presents and other people were buying them for you. Now you get yet another bottle of aftershave or a pack of bath bombs and have to hand over to the kids all the cool stuff you would have murdered for at age 10. So in essence we all want to rewrite Christmas and dump all the modern things we hate in favour of everything good we remember from our own childhoods. If you have good memories of what Christmas was like when you were young and not all of us do.

Anyway, I think there are still some features of the modern event that might be worth keeping in your imaginary Christmas makeover and one of these is … the Christmas letter. Thanks to the deluge of computers we've all been getting for Christmases past, not to mention cheap printers, bundled software and IT skills courses urged upon us until they are coming out of our ears, it is now possible for almost anyone to construct and include with their Christmas card a bit of an update on their doings over the past year.

Now before you start, I'm well aware that there are examples of the genre whose merits remain somewhat mysterious. Do we really need to know that Auntie Jean had her hip done in March, won £3.65 on the National Lottery in May and went on holiday to Faleraki in October. No is the simple answer. On the other hand however this may be all the contact you have since she now lives in Hartlepool, a bit off the beaten track for most A9 motorists and in any case neither of you can think of a good reason for phoning each other up.

The point of the Christmas letter is simply this - to remind you that there are other members of the species you are related to, grew up with, went to college with or tripped over in some other way along the path of life that you really should keep some contact with. A simple Christmas card illustrating Santa's adventures with a St Bernard and a barrel of brandy with a barely readable scrawl inside frankly tells you nothing about the sender, other than that they have poor taste in Christmas cards and not very clear handwriting. The inclusion of a Christmas letter - even if it is photocopied, even if it looks like an accident in a font factory, even if it is addressed personally to you when you know that another 300 close personal friends have got the very same thing, even in all these circumstances - does give you something of a glimpse into the last 12 months for people you ought to care about.

And to be really successful, a Christmas letter is not recommended to deal only with lumbago, dieting and grandson Shane's first tooth. What we really want to know is - how was it for you? Did the year past see you ticking off more of your life list items (climbed Everest, published my novel, found love at last, learned Italian and took up indoor point to point hot air ballooning) or have things been hard. Perhaps the last year has been more about illness, injury, redundancy and relationship problems. Or perhaps, like for most of us, things have been a bit mixed. Some of it worked out and some of it didn't. Some things you managed and others you screwed up. And it's in circumstances like these - when not everything has gone exactly swimmingly - that the whole point of keeping in touch at Christmas resides. When you get a Christmas letter like this what it's asking you to do is not just sit back and think thank goodness that didn't happen to me, but to pick up the phone and make a Christmas letter into a Christmas conversation.

Writing the Christmas letter is of course also a good time to sit down and review your own year too. Amidst all the harassment of buying presents, organising whose family are going to host Christmas dinner and worrying about what on earth you can get your loved one that is likely to be treasured beyond 26th December, it is worth finding a few minutes to sit down and reflect on how it's all gone in your own life. And why. In the old days we used to say "count your blessings, name them one by one", now it's more "always look on the bright side of life". However you express it there are bound to be things to be grateful for, relationships to value and memories to value. And at Christmas time, who do you think we might be grateful to? Answers on the back of a Christmas letter.

Reasons to be Cheerful Part 4

Oh dear, it's January again - surely the most miserable month. Christmas has come and gone. Presents you tried to look so grateful for on the day are now eaten, broken, lost, used up, purloined, abandoned or sometimes still sitting in the corner while you try to work out what they're for. Too many turkey dinners and mince pies have done their worst as the bathroom scales now testify. Too much toasting of the New Year has produced its own inevitable side effects boosting sales of Anadin and carpet shampoo. Now we're into a new year which includes all the fun of getting back to work, paying for Christmas past and coping with the worst of winter weather to come - all without any imminent fun or festivities to look forward to…

So, at this time of year, perhaps more than any other, what we need are reasons to be cheerful. Ian Drury, who of course owns the copyright on this concept suggested among other things:

The juice of the carrot, the smile of the parrot,
A little drop of claret - anything that rocks
Elvis and Scotty, days when I ain't spotty,
Sitting on the potty - curing small pox

And while these are certainly good and sensible reasons, there might still be scope for coming up with a few more of our own. And what better time of year for it. So here goes with my top three reasons to be cheerful…

1. Things that went wrong last year won't be going to go wrong in exactly the same way this year.

This follows the principle that lightening never strikes twice - if it got you once it can't get you again. Now, readers who got the Guinness Book of Records for Christmas will undoubtedly point out this isn't true citing Roy Sullivan who was struck a record 7 times between 1942 and his death in 1983. However in reply to this, the fact is that Sullivan's injuries were slightly different every time. From losing the nail off his big toe, to having his hair set on fire and suffering burns to his shoulder, every occasion was slightly different. So I would still maintain that you are now totally immune from that particular car crash, row with your spouse, flooding, house fire, dose of the flu, foot in mouth moment or tax bill that plagued the year just gone. Something similar may well crop up but not the exact same. I hope you find that a comforting thought.

2. Things that look dead can revive.

January is probably the month in which things look absolutely deadest. Just before Christmas we lifted the last of the potatoes, beetroot and parsnips and not bad they were too. But now, after a bit of a dig over, the garden is looking absolutely blank - much like the expression on my face when asked to help with son number two's maths homework in fact. However, whether you spend all day every day worrying about it or utterly ignore the whole thing, in a couple of months life will start to get going again completely without your help or intervention. Sadly of course this includes docken and thistles, so some intervention is required, but without that bit of rising sap and the natural kick start we call Spring nothing you nor I could do would make a whit of difference. So, in the ebb and flow of things, it can be a mistake to consign something to the compost heap, thinking it's dead, when there might be life in the old dog yet. Relationships, ambitions, high hopes - they might just be playing hard to get and need a bit of TLC. As the Desiderata puts it "Keep interested in your own career, however humble; it is a real possession in the changing fortunes of time." Or if your tastes run to something a bit less grandiose, how about Frank Sinatra singing: "So any time your gettin' low 'stead of lettin' go Just remember that ant … Oops there goes another rubber tree plant."

3. A new year is a chance for a new beginning

While I wouldn't dare to mention new year resolutions, have you noticed how absolutely stuffed life is with opportunities to have another go? Every single 24 hours, 7 days and 12 months - not to mention birthdays, anniversaries and yom kippur - you get to begin again, try to put previous muck ups behind you and have another go. We're like the man who was painting his house and found he was about one whole tin short. What he did have however was plenty of thinners so he set about eking things out accordingly. Of course from a deep shade of mahogany on the front, things got lighter and lighter all the way round till the final side was only slightly darker than the colour you go when the sun's out on Country Show day. In desperation (and with his wife due back from the shops any minute) he looked up to heaven and cried out in despair, "Oh Lord. It looks terrible. What should I do?" in reply to which a voice boomed out, "Repaint my son and thin no more!" So New Year is traditionally a time for reassessing where you're at and wondering if it's where you want to be. Maybe you need to get a new tin in a new shade and paint the house a different colour. My favourite refocusing aid this year is John Ortberg's "It all goes back in the box" supplied by my friend Jan at the Mustard Seed bookshop. Ortberg reminds us that when the game of life is over everything goes back in the box and none of it survives except those things with eternal significance. So all the store we set by material gain, power and influence and good looks (especially the later) may really be a waste of time if we haven't got the longer term priorities right. And when better than the New Year to think it over…

So despite indications to the contrary (and any mention of Grumpy Old Men) I'm hoping to retain a bit of good humour and general optimism through the months to come while simultaneously running on the spot, shampooing the rug and sending out for extra supplies of paracetamol. Happy New Year!

Watch out - Danger Man about

Larry Walker was a man with a mission. His lifetime ambition was to learn to fly but, refused entry to the air force on account of poor eyesight, he had to find another way. So he connected 45 weather balloons to a garden seat and strapped himself in along with some sandwiches, a few beers and a pellet gun. Unfortunately, when his friends cut the cord, instead of hovering at about 30 feet as he had planned, he just kept on going, finally levelling off at over 16,000 feet. By this time he was a bit nervous about shooting anything so he just hung on, slowly drifting into Los Angeles airport airspace. After several hours, when he did eventually decide to pop a few balloons, he only floated down far enough to get caught in some power lines from where he was eventually rescued. When asked why he did it, Larry replied, "A man can't just sit there."

Now apart from the fact that some people are basically crazy and that weather balloons ought not to be on general sale, is there anything to be learned from Larry's amazing adventures? I think there might be. We live in an increasingly risk averse society. Risk assessments are all the rage followed by comprehensive warnings and detailed measures to minimise all possible ill effects of anything that might go wrong. And when something bad happens it's the authorities who should have prevented it who get the blame rather than those responsible for the mayhem in the first place. In general terms unnecessary risks should be course be reduced and nobody would defend dangerous practices - thinking back to the number of months my own mother spent in bed as a result of a lifting injury, I have to be say that. But on the other hand there are problems with waging war on all possible risks for at least two good reasons, namely (1) Life is risky and (2) a bit of danger is good for you.

Having recently driven 300 miles in a single stretch, at night, in the rain, I feel fairly well acquainted with needless risks and so am definitely in favour of safer roads, slower cars and better lighting etc. What I don't need is protection from something that is not a real risk in the first place and which, if I am determined enough to make it into a risk, then I deserve every ill effect I get. You know what I mean. There should be no need for the manufacturers of weather balloons and garden chairs to warn their customers that these two items should not be connected while the balloons are inflated and the chair is occupied. And in case you think I'm joking, this very afternoon I had occasion to buy a metronome (don't ask why) which was completely devoid of musical instructions but did contain the following helpful note: "The metronome is made of plastic and iron materials and should not be thrown about or towards a person since it is dangerous". Really. That is so frustrating because that was exactly why I bought it. It's dead handy to have something nice and heavy to lob at intruders and I've often thought a metronome would be perfect. Sadly, I'll now have to look for something else - maybe a garden seat. So we don't need a label on the hot tap saying this water is hot or on a bag of nuts saying this bag contains nuts.

Secondly however, there's another wee issue hinted at by Larry's laconic reply. Not only is life dangerous, but human nature needs a bit of danger to keep things interesting. Bungee jumping, sky diving, caving, motor sports, dinghy racing, January Sales. Need I say more. Larry was fed up sitting in his garden seat moaning about all the things he couldn't do and one day decided to get up - or perhaps sit down - and do something about it. One of last year's bestsellers was "The Dangerous Book for Boys" Look at the great video at http://uk.youtube. com/watch?v=c5PSdBWvx8s to find out why. My own meagre nod in this direction was to paddle in an open canoe 60 miles down the River Spey last year with our younger teenager boy. Did we stay dry? Nope. Did we enjoy it and learn a bit about ourselves and each other? Absolutely.

So some danger is not only inevitable but recommended. Like a muscle that needs to push against resistance to develop, we all need something in life to push against to grow. But that something needs to be the right sort of something. Bullying in the workplace is not it, nor is picking cockles in Morecambe Bay while the tide comes in. So as well as regulation we also need room to test and measure ourselves - perhaps increasingly as the years advance. Along with proper health and safety legislation maybe we also need a little bit of craziness now and again to wake everybody up. Maybe next year's publishing sensation should be the Dangerous Book for Grown Ups. Anyway, hats off to Larry Walker. The theory was ok, just next time keep the tether attached!

Rosy does the Business

One of our 2008 New Year's resolutions in the Cowan household has been to recycle a bit more. We are of course concerned, as we certainly ought to be, about climate change, rising sea levels, flooding in Bangladesh, the possible disappearance of Tahiti and the need for improved flood defences in Junction Road. Sadly, however, I have to admit that the main reason for this change of heart is none of the above. It's that other rising tide that has spurred us into action - the relentlessly rising number of unwanted, unsolicited and unappreciated marketing catalogues that drop through our letter box almost every day. The postman's van is full of them, our waste paper bins are stuffed with them, our black bags bulge with them and the welcome mat beneath our letter box is flattened by them. So this year they're at least being put to some good use and are heading for recycling rather than landfill.

I expect you know the kind of thing I mean. They are variously for women's clothing, supermarket promotions, bathroom makeovers, women's clothing, sports equipment, marine supplies, women's clothing, loft conversions and - did I mention women's clothing? Anyway they are mostly junk and I've decided I'd rather have them repulped into something more useful, like chip wrappers than simply dumped in a big hole to pose a problem for our offspring in years to come.

However…just as an exception to prove the rule, we recently got an unsolicited marketing catalogue that was not a total waste of paper. In fact it was great fun and far more entertaining than almost anything else that's dropped through the letter box this month - even including tax demands and VAT forms which we always try to enjoy as much as possible. It was - to name names - the Rosy Nieper t-shirts catalogue. Sadly for Rosy and chums it's unlikely I'll be buying anything from them, but I really did enjoy the catalogue. It is, you won't be surprised to hear, full of t-shirts. Not that the t-shirt itself is a particularly funny garment, say compared to clown shoes or baggy drawers, but it does adapt very well to having funny or witty slogans on it and this is where Rosy does the business. None of your "I'm with stupid" or "My Dad went to London and all he got me was this lousy T-shirt". No - mostly they are actually quite good. For example…

For fat-and-proud-of-it people we have the four stages of Life: "You believe in Santa, You don't believe in Santa, You are Santa, You look like Santa." Movie fans can enjoy a pair of red shoes and the slogan "Auntie Em - Hate you, Hate Kansas, Took the dog, Dorothy". Internet geeks who think the whole world is interested in what they had for breakfast get "Enough about me - let's talk about my BLOG" (So true, isn't it - so sadly, sadly true…) For kitchen nightmare cooks we have a tub of lovely smooth creamy custard next to a lumpy disaster zone and the slogans "Birds custard…blokes custard". Great. My personal favourite however is for the birdwatcher in your life. In a nightmarish scene which would liven up Bill Oddie's next TV bore-athon no end, an owl up a tree is swearing at a twitcher above the slogan "Irritable Owl Syndrome". Fantastic. It's what t-shirts were invented for.

And Rosy doesn't even have the total market. With a heady mixture of wounded male pride, post feminist ennui and subtle hints of Zen I noticed a harried looking bloke the other day wearing one that said "If a man said something in the forest where there were no women to hear him, would he still be wrong?" You feel you could pretty much guess what the rest of his life was like just from that one remark.

In an age when you might think a lot of the fun has gone out of life - all we hear about are financial crises, military crises, economic crises and environmental crises - the sight of a reasonably funny slogan adorning somebody wandering past you in the high street is surely something to be thankful for. Even despite the fact that to read it properly you may have to spend several seconds staring fixedly at the chest of whatever shapely creature might be wearing it. I know, it's a rotten job but somebody's got to do it.

So anyway, what's it all about? How have we gone from a simple Levi logo and some artwork of two horses trying to pull a pair of jeans in half to using garments to say whatever you want about life, the universe and everything? Probably like the wheel, fire and wood chip wallpaper it's one of those things that maybe no one person can take all the credit for. The reason it works is because people want to be heard. On the one hand we live in an age of rampant individualism but on the other you keep getting the feeling that nothing you say frankly makes any difference. At least if you can slap something on your chest and wander round the shops you will be saying something and somebody might notice. It might be banal or offensive or meaningless or in Rosy's case (and my opinion) quite funny -but at least you're saying something. It used to be the case that "wearing your heart on your sleeve" was thought to be kind of bad form - something that showed you up as lacking proper reserve and gravitas. Now everything is a fashion statement - including statements slapped on a piece of fashion. You may not like them, agree with them or personally wear them but it's hard to ignore them. Personally I think they can definitely brighten a dreary winter's day trailing round the shops. So go on punk - make my day - wear something funny.

And the Capital of Venezuela is….

There was a time when the need to prove your superior wit, wisdom and all round topdogishness against all comers was the preserve of the young and foolish. Nowadays, while the young and foolish are still at it and probably will be until all human life expires, the world has changed in one important respect. In 1905 the average life expectancy of a British male was about 47 and 50 for females. Now it's more like 75 for men and 80 for women. So more people are more able for longer and that also means we need an outlet for our competitive urges much later in life.

So where might such an outlet be found when you can no longer cope with Saturday morning five a side and they won't let you have a javelin of your own? What we need is something that allows men and women of … how can I put it … middle years … to engage in as much competition as they like in a safe and comfortable environment, testing their mettle against their peers and satisfying all competitive urges. Well, there is a perfect solution - it's called the pub quiz.

Now, pubs have been around for a long time but pub quizzes seem to be a more modern phenomenon. Exactly how they started is probably a mystery, but I think we can take some educated guesses - exactly as you would when asked the name of the Greek god of wisdom and crafts. Firstly, I imagine whenever blokes have got together with a glass in front of them (and although many women take part in pub quizzes somehow it still seems a rather blokish phenomenon) questions have been asked. Sometimes these are restricted to the straightforward - "Whose round is it anyway?" but then you also get the "Can you settle an argument …" type of situation that invariably seems to have started with said argument happening in the pub. Now, you might think there are more useful and worthwhile things to talk about than the final score in the Falkirk v St Mirren Cup Final of 12th December 1993 but nevertheless someone, somewhere thinks they know and someone else propping up the bar right next to them thinks they're wrong. (Just to satisfy your curiosity, Falkirk won three nil).

So the necessary components seem to be:

- insufficient gainful employment
- reasonable amounts of liquid refreshment and
- too many people who think they know more than anybody else

And where these three things come together is, of course, in the pub…

So, given these basic ingredients, and assuming we have premises, participants, a well stocked bar and too much free time, what's needed next is someone to put the thing on a proper footing and add the final ingredients. Most importantly we need a question master or mistress. Now, on the one hand this might seem like a thankless task - much like being a football referee in fact - but clearly there must be hidden benefits or nobody would volunteer. On the downside you used to have to spend hours and hours pouring over reference books, statistical archives, Encyclopaedia Britannica and Who's Who or else making up music clips of hits from the 60s and picture sheets with flags of the world but with computer technology and the internet, now even that has become a great deal easier. At the latest count Google gives over 1,210,000 hits for "pub quiz" which even allowing for casual references probably still means more questions out there than can be either asked or answered in several long lifetimes of drinking and arguing - even for the thirstiest and most contrary amongst us (you know who you are!). On the upside, as question master you have the chance to outsmart everyone else in the company as if you made up all the questions and answers out of your head and have plenty more where those came from. While we all know this isn't likely to be true, nobody thinks of Magnus Magnusson, Bamber Gascoigne and Jeremy Paxman as particularly thick and all pub quiz question maestros hope that some of that aura of intelligence might stick to them as well.

Next up, the assorted rabble of know alls, dunces, would be football experts and second hand car salesmen who find themselves down the pub need to be organised into teams if some meaningful competition is to be entered into. This process comes in two parts - one easy and one very difficult. The easy part is actually making up your team, getting sat down in your chosen corner and getting a pencil and paper in front of you, preferably on the last remaining bit of table not sopping with a heady mixture of lager spillage and damp fragments of cheese and onion. The hard part is choosing your team name. I have seen teams whose toughest challenge of the entire night was without doubt the choice between Wally's Winners and Fat and Forty. I'll leave it to your imagination which option is more likely to accurately describe typical pub quiz competitors.

So, with a question master, participants raring to go, a score sheet with all obscene team names tastefully corrected and drinks on the table, let battle commence. And our first round is on … famous musical moments from the world of opera, followed by popular soap stars and their best known characteristics. Have you noticed that pub quiz questions have a particular flavour to them, often falling into one of two categories: things you stand almost no chance of knowing unless you were there at the time, and things you know perfectly well but are embarrassed to admit to. So you might get asked "Why did Toscanini put down his baton and walk out in the middle of Act III during the premiere of Puccini's Turandot at La Scala in 1926?" (Answer - because Puccini had died leaving it unfinished) or "Who plays the cheese-loving karaoke queen, Heather Trott in Eastenders?" (Answer Cheryl Ferguson). In the one case, only holiday makers who happened to be in Milan on the night in question have a chance and in the other case, all those that actually know should hang their heads in shame.

And so the night wears on. Participants grow more and more either excited or depressed as their level of confidence dictates, till some are driven to put down any old rubbish in the hope of winning the booby prize - a pair of left handed scissors for the answer that makes the question master giggle the most. And what does it all amount to? Well, actually not a bad night out in most cases. Sometimes you're surprised by the hidden talents of your friends, often a bit disappointed in your own performance ("I knew that" you hear yourself saying even when you patently didn't as the score sheet testifies) and occasionally you might even learn something of benefit.

On the other hand, while it's all good fun, personally I have never found much specific self improvement in finding out that The Bedrock Bugle and The Daily Slab were the newspapers read by Fred Flintstone. I guess what I'm really looking for is a pub quiz that might help me find out more useful stuff I can put into practice somewhere other than inside the pub. Like where I left my mobile phone and how to pay less tax. If you find a pub quiz that answers questions like that, please let me know…

What actually is in a name?

I'm sure it's not just because it's Spring but for whatever reason there seems to be lots of babyness about. Friends and relatives are expecting, others have just had and the number of babies and toddlers trooping out to our Sunday School and crèche seems to have taken a sudden hike. New babies of course bring with them all sorts of excitement, stress and new dilemmas but I wonder if pretty near the top in all three categories comes the perennial - what on earth are we going to call it? Apparently baby names are seriously subject to fashion and every year a new crop of wannabees slug it out with the old favourites for top spot. Right now Jack, Lewis and Callum are apparently doing particularly well in Scotland along with Sophie, Emma and Erin. Not far behind come the slightly less conventional Harley (a boy) Niamh (a girl) and Morgan (maybe could be either).

Now, children's names are a highly personal thing but surely one overriding imperative must apply - do not to call your offspring something everyone will live to regret! You know - the sort of thing that provokes a wave of stifled giggling when the teacher asks if Helen Back is present or later in life results in a stunned silence as we slowly process the combination of surname Flay and forename Sue. In fact I would like to propose that all prospective parents stand in front of the mirror and repeat three times both slowly and at normal speed what the new arrival stands in danger of being stuck with for life, first with the current surname, then all possible alternatives, just to be sure. Failure to do so could result in something too obscene to be pronounced in normal conversation and in that case should carry a mandatory prison sentence followed by five years statutory renaming of both parents with something even more appalling at their child's discretion.

And, if you're wondering where all this is coming from, I recently stumbled across the fabulous "Potty, Fartwell and Knob: Extraordinary but true names of British People" by Russell Ash and ever since both gentle sniggering and loud guffaws have been echoing round the house. How the amazing Mr. Ash managed to put together such a treasury I have no idea but, however it was done, the results are truly amazing - no doubt hideous for the victims but, it must be said, fantastic for us. Setting aside those too obscene to reproduce in a family column, you have to question the sanity of those parents responsible for Gladys Friday, Pete Bog or Page Turner. It's astonishing. Along with these, we find the equally wonderful Hester Snogs, Hairy Head, Cliff Edge and amazingly not only Ben but also Eileen Dover. The musical section gives us Carrie Oke, Mike Stand and Mel Oddy and for a more modern feel, I. Tunes and I. Pod! The food chapter includes Hans Sandwich, Annie Seed, Basil Leaf, Chris P. Bacon and Walter Cress and under human geography we can find May Fair, Hyde Park, Nan Tucket and even Windsor Castle. In fact it just goes on and on. Ferris Wheeler is followed by Luke Warm, Joss Stick and the unbelievable Minty Badger. And apparently, it is all true as dates of birth and parish of origin are given on each and every occasion.

But in case you think this sort of thing appears in print but rarely in life, my mate Andy insists he was taught history by Norman Conquest, one family member once worked with Hazel Nut, another claims the acquaintance of Holly Wood and a former fellow student insists he clerked a man called Forest Branch into hospital. Post christening stress disorder I imagine. And for a final up to date example, I've just noticed that the Homes Editor for Good Housekeeping Magazine right now happens to be the hapless Anne-Lisa De'Eath. Amazing - you could hardly make it up. By the way do not ask why I was reading Good Housekeeping in the first place…

Ok - so where are we up to? Some folk have unlikely and kind of amusing names. So far, so funny, but is there anything more that can be said - apart from the fact that parents simply can't be trusted - which most of us know already. For example, does the choice of name you're given have any bearing on your future character and career prospects? In some respects, I suppose it must. Is anyone called Jay Walker going to get a job in road safely? Or maybe the opposite also applies and people might be drawn to occupations that seem to suit. My wife's two physics teachers at school were Mr. Watt and Mr. Power. Perfect. On the other hand her dance teachers were Mr. and Mrs. Stiff - possibly not so fitting. It seems we must think there is some connection between names and characteristics since in the English language world (or at least that part of it I grew up in) certain names have found their way into popular usage. For example we have as happy as Larry, big hearted Arthur, knowledgeable Archie and even Gorgeous George. But are people called Joy any happier than those called Mona? Are people called Laurie more likely to work in transportation and those called Sue more likely to end up in court? And in any case, would changing your name make any difference or as Darth Vadar kept telling Luke Skywalker (both names which seem strangely fitted to their line of work) "It is your destiny".

So, what are we as parents to do about it given the alarming level of responsibility entrusted to us? Can I suggest - rule one - steer clear of any names with double meanings, also bearing shortened forms in mind. I hope I don't need to spell this out - suffice it to say that guys called William and Richard probably know where we're coming from here. Rule two - if you must call your daughter Henrietta, you must also absolutely forbid her going out with Peter Bone (and all such similar suitors). But finally, remember - your kids will take far more into life from hanging around with you than they ever will from any possible name you land them with. Get that right and maybe your choice of name may not be so crucial. But even bearing that in mind I still don't think that Penny Black was a good idea...

Confessions of a Bookshelf Browser

Nosiness takes many forms. For example, it's a fact that lots of Orkney households have a pair of binoculars sat by the kitchen window. Is it for bird watching (maybe), looking out for a passing bus just in time to tear down the road and catch it (possible) or is it, (more probably) for keeping an eye on unusual neighbourhood goings on? What is that man doing with 27 car tyres, a sheet of green plastic, a flagpole, a wheelbarrow and a box of fireworks? Is it modern art or Orkney's first moon shot? Quick, get the binoculars. Let's have a closer look.

This is all relatively innocent of course. On the more serious side, I believe there are folk that actually make a career of going through other people's bins on the hunt for anything worthwhile - like credit card details for example. And what about computer hacking? The reason why we're all up in arms about the loss of government data is not just the cost of 2 CDs. It's the fact that somebody, somewhere will wonder what's on them, stick them in their home PC, discover 3 million personal records and think there must a market for that sort of thing. Like I said - nosiness.

Anyway, now's the time to fess up. I am just as nosy as the next one, it's just that my nosiness takes a slightly unusual form. I like browsing other people's bookshelves. It's true. I have sought help but there aren't any suitable support groups and I've yet to find any medication that really works. Anyway, the fact is that you can find out far more about your friends by scanning what's on their bookshelves than you ever would from merely separating their bank statement from the remains of last week's fish supper. If you want to know what really makes them tick skip the skip and have a browse among the books.

So, point one - are there any books besides the 1977 Guinness Book of Records and a couple of college leftovers? Answer "no" and you either have to remain in the dark or else get your rubber gloves on just before black bag day. Answer "yes" and we're on our way.

Point two - what's actually there? Lots or a little? Any recurrent themes or completely random? Coffee table books or books you would actually read? Fact or fiction - though in the case of modern celebrity biographies it can be pretty hard to tell the difference. Are they all quite recent, predominantly from more than 20 years ago or a healthy mixture? And is it all reading material or are we mainly just looking at the pictures here? Now clearly, on all these counts, the point is to put your deerstalker on, get out your long wiggly pipe and start drawing some conclusions. For example, on the evidence of books alone, you might conclude that your friend is a retired racing driver now interested in hair dressing, an expert in SAS survival techniques but still with a tender, romantic side who dabbles in embroidery. Good. This is definitely showing up a side you never suspected. Unfortunately, you then discover that the book collection mainly derives from what was left in granny and grandad's attic when the house was cleared last month. Hmm. Back to the drawing board.

Actually, of course, you're probably going to be on pretty shaky ground drawing much in the way of conclusions just from this approach, but luckily there is another, simpler way, namely, do they have some of the same books as you? I'm always fascinated to find some of my own book collection moonlighting on somebody else's shelves and I immediately find myself jumping to probably quite wild conclusions. For example, I do not believe anyone who has read and enjoyed Three Men in a Boat can be wholly bad. Similarly anyone who had read and understood A Brief History of Time is not a good person to get into a physics argument with. Incidentally I'm sure there's a good publishing opportunity for A Timely History of Briefs but no doubt that's why I'm not in the book trade...Anyway, once you spot something familiar, your immediate next thought is to wonder what they thought of it and was it for the same reasons as you. Fascinating - as Mr. Spock was prone to say.

But what about your own book collection?. As I'm sure you'd guess, Loose Talk gets a constant flow of letters asking for timely social advice and this week (as it happens) we had one specifically on this subject. "Dear Loose Talk, I have recently started a new job and have some work colleagues coming round for supper on Tuesday. What sort of reading material should I leave out to make the best impression? Yours etc. J.R.S." Well J, space precludes a full treatise. However John le Carré never goes wrong, Harry Potter stops you from seeming too highbrow, Being Jordan should not be displayed to males between 12 and 93 and anything by Gary Larson always raises a laugh. But perhaps you should keep your History of Negligées in a locked drawer. The most important point however is to have something around for nosy bookshelf browsers like me. We'll thank you for it. For as the famous Groucho put it so well, "Outside of a dog, a book is a man's best friend. Inside of a dog it's too dark to read."

Accidents will happen

(thank goodness)

"Serendipity" is such a cool word. Not only does it have quite a nice ring when you say it out loud, but it happens to have a fantastic meaning - full, as they say, of eastern promise. Just in case you haven't come across it before, serendipity is defined by my dictionary as "the faculty of making fortunate discoveries by accident". I ask you, what could be better?

Life in the 21st century seems to be so hedged around by plans. Proper planning prevents poor performance, we're told. Hope for the best but plan for the worst, they say. Council departments have to plan as if their very lives depended on it (which perhaps they do) in search of better services. Along the way we have to wonder if all the time and money spent planning were to be put into doing what probably most of the team already know needs to be done, might there not be a better outcome - and I speak as a former employee with some responsibility for planning!

On a more personal level, life coaches tell us that if we want to achieve our life goals, we need to make more positive plans complete with appropriate short term goals, mid term rewards and longer term envisioning. How on earth do you expect to (a) climb Mt. Kilimanjaro (b) achieve grand master status in origami or (c) lose six stone if you don't make the necessary plans, for goodness sake? It's not going to happen by accident!

But, there of course lies the rub. Of course it's not going to happen by accident, but on the other hand, lots of other cool stuff might. Which brings us back to our word of the week. Can you imagine what life would be like if everything was planned and nothing happened by accident? You would know exactly what you were going to eat / drink / wear / do and indeed not do for the entire rest of your life. No fun surprises, no intriguing chance encounters, no unexpected stumbling on a great book, singer or travel destination. Everything prescribed, determined and predestined (apologies to the Calvinists among us) with no room for randomness and unpredictability. What a boring world! It might be somewhat safer, which of course would be quite a benefit, but think what we would be missing. How many of your favourite books, musicians or indeed friends did you plan to discover and like? I would guess approximately none. Things happen in an unexpected manner and therein lies the glory and the beauty of life. You bump into someone in the cinema queue, strike up a conversation and there you are. Bob's your uncle. A friend for life. You notice an article about Katmandu in a magazine at the dentist's, read a few lines and discover you really fancy it. Cancel the B&B in Bognor - let's go somewhere interesting.

And this is not just hypothetical. It really happens. Let me illustrate. From time to time I (and perhaps I'm not alone in this) find myself with a little time to spare while waiting for my nearest and dearest. Sound familiar? Ok - no sexism here - sometimes she has to hang around a bit waiting for me. Though definitely not as often. Anyway, we were due to rendezvous one evening and having arrived at the prearranged time i.e. about 45 minutes before actually required, I sat in the car, tried to content myself and stuck on the radio. Instead of screeching valkyries on Radio 3, the Westminster Hour on Radio 4, Friday Night is Music Night on Radio 2 (preserve us) or (especially) The Best of Drum and Bass on Radio One, it happened (by accident) to be Radio Scotland - and a reasonably enjoyable mix of traditional and contemporary American folk hosted by the enthusiastic Dean Freedman. Ok - all well and good and therefore maybe not a total waste of time. But then the real serendipity kicked in. His guest star that evening (for one night only) was the amazing and fantastic Christine Lavin (catch her at www.christinelavin.com). We were then treated to a truly sublime mix of wit, poetry, humour, insight and great tunes such that not only was I content to wait but when said life partner emerged I was in an all forgiving mood and hardly grumpy at all. Which really was unexpected.

Now, here I could take 150 words to regale you with what I actually enjoyed so much about Ms Lavin's performance - but that's not really the point. The fact is that I bumped into her (metaphorically speaking) by accident. And the fact that I have now actually parted with money and downloaded some of the best songs of the night from the Apple iTunes web store at 79p a time is proof of the impact.

Now, far be it from this column not to appreciate all the time and effort you are putting in to further your career, get some qualifications or make an all round improvement by dint of sheer hard work and - yes - planning. Of course it's essential. All I'm sticking up for is the other side of the coin. We also need some unexpectedness in life to really make the fun begin. So a plague on all your planning I say and let's all drink to a touch of out and out randomness now and then. Not sure what to toast it with? Live dangerously. Stick your hand in the fridge and pull out something random!

Olympics over? Feeling left out?

Help is at hand

It's over at last. The cyclists, sailors, athletes and hockey players have all gone home, sports commentators have returned to their normal dreary lives commenting on the 2.15 from Haydock Park and the Bird's Nest Stadium has been returned to its previous role as the world's largest speciality soup emporium. Such Olympic interest as anyone can still summon up is now apparently focussed on London 2012 given that Finstown's bid was eventually unsuccessful and Heddle Hill will have to remain unregenerated for the foreseeable future. So if the Olympic fire is still burning in your veins, sadly, you now have limited options. Basically you can either choose to relive as much of our recent glory as possible by sitting glued to Youtube clips of Chris Hoy all day (and why not) or try to get as worked up as possible over the odds of Britain pushing its way even higher up the medals table hence proving against all the odds that we are not as totally rubbish at everything as we've been led to believe for the last thirty years.

All well and good if that's what you fancy but I can't help feeling both alternatives are verging a bit on the passive side. After all that straining, striving and of course sweating, I definitely feel something a bit more active is called for. Now before you jump to any conclusions I'm not about to recommend actual exercise with a view to becoming potential Olympians ourselves. Let's stay in the real world here. My own hopes of sporting glory never got beyond a small bronze (coloured) badge indicating third place in the Central Region Under 15 boys 50m breast stroke 1972. Your may of course have achieved a great deal more but let's face it, for most of us, if it was going to happen it would have happened a long time ago. So how can we armchair Olympians feel a bit more actively involved while we twiddle our thumbs and wait for 2012?

Well, I think the key to this lies in one of what for me at least was the number one surprise of Beijing. We were apparently surprised at how well the Chinese managed the whole thing - though I don't see why we should have been. Look at the Great Wall and consider how long it takes most of us to put up a teeny wee bit of garden fence. Secondly

90

we were surprised at coming so high up the pecking order of nations. Apparently since the Olympics doesn't involve the traditional Scotland / England rivalry the key thing is to whack the Aussies which it seems we did with ease. Well done us. But the third and greatest surprise was the growing number of unlikely sports that seem to be making it onto the official Olympic list.

We are already pretty used to the fact that what we used to call ping pong and play at youth club has now become supersonic, long distance, high velocity table tennis played by young people with faster reactions than rattlesnakes and an unending supply of dry polo shirts. But what about BMX cycling? Until I actually saw the competition I had no idea it involved racing on BMXs. I suppose I expected it to involve hanging around outside the chip shop attempting the odd trick for passers-by which is all I'd ever seen BMXs used for before. And ladies beach volleyball. What can I say? Or, to be more accurate, what can I say that's printable and doesn't consign me to the spare bedroom until I've apologised profusely and cleared up any misunderstanding. Then there's synchronised swimming, last seen in black and white in a series of Busby Berkeley spectaculars accompanied by selections from the best of Irving Berlin. What's that all about?

So you get the idea. There seems no end to the weird stuff that can end up as an Olympic sport - and that, ladies and gentlemen is what may give us some reason for hope. So you want to get involved, bring back a few medals and get an open topped bus ride round your own home town. But you'd rather achieve this without having to get up at 5.30 am every day including Sunday and would prefer not to have to invest in a pair of size 63 lycra shorts. Ok - here's the deal. Invent a new sport that you're already good at and get it onto the Olympic list! Fantastic. You won't need to train since you're already at the peak of your performance, can choose whatever dress code you fancy (personally I favour the comfortable and stain resistant individual inflatable sumo suit) and will be able to knock spots off all comers, Aussies and Chinese included.

But what to choose? Indoor 4 x 100 fish supper consumption could be costly without appropriate sponsorship from the Happy Haddock. Mixed doubles Ebay shopping would be good but might involve extending the garage to accommodate all the junk we pick up. Left handed mobile phone texting could be worth considering except for a definite youth and gender bias. Hmmm... Let me think…What am I better at than anyone else I know, doesn't cost much, can be done equally well from a prone position, requires no special equipment and doesn't tire you out? Does the fact that significant other always refers to this as the "grumpy old man" column give me an idea? You bet it does. With only four years to go I'd better get some practice in. Why does nobody ever put the TV remote back where it should be? How about turning the lights off once in a while - do you think we have shares in Powergen? Has anybody seen my car keys? Do we really need another set of miniature village ornaments??? Etc. etc. Whoa - way to go. I'm getting better already.

Say hullo to Robbie ...

- and goodbye to domestic strife

It's here, you know. Not as soon as some predicted though long before I for one expected. It doesn't look much like you'd think but there's no telling what it might turn into. Your Granddad wouldn't have believed it, and to be honest I don't quite believe it myself. Your children will probably take it for granted in a few years time. What is it? Believe it or not, it's the arrival of useful, practical, domestic robots! Yes, really. The concept of robots isn't itself too weird nowadays but so far they've been mostly occupied in painting graffiti on the sides of Xsara Picasso cars. Of course they probably build the things as well but in either case, so far, they've been safely stuck in factories far away from me. Until now.

The problem was that Family Cowan has recently been on the look out for a hoover to replace the mangled remains we've been valiantly lugging round the house for the last few years. The current model weighs a ton, spits out more than it sucks, gets totally clogged even on the meagre remains of a teenage coke-and-crisps-fest and directs all remaining power to sucking the hose completely flat till not a speck can get more than half way up the tube. Then what started as a suck ends up as a wheeze (from the hoover) and a howl of frustration (from the hooverer). So something - as they say - had to be done. Now, our normal approach would be to wander aimlessly round the shops, surf aimlessly round the internet then shuffle aimlessly round the house looking for a catalogue that has now vanished, taking with it the hoover offer of a lifetime. Finally we manage to galvanise ourselves into a decision only once the mountain of dirt becomes greater than our powers of procrastination and we get the bally thing ordered.

This time however the issue was further complicated when a bit of web searching turned up the fact that you can really and truly, right now buy an actual robot hoover. Wow. Amazing. People definitely have them and use them and seem to think they're ok. So far none have run amok, hoovered up the dog, run off with the wife or shredded the Persian hearth rug we got from John Lewis's with our compensation money last year. So far so good, but I bet they cost a fortune. Well, even more amazing is the fact that they come in at pretty much what a normal

93

replacement hoover would cost. That's to say there is a fancier, flashier one with radar, sonar, GPS, VHF, mapping software and a rev counter that costs over a thousand quid but that was off the agenda before it even got on. So it's available, affordable, apparently useable and "in the shops now" as they say. What could be better?

Well, even better is the fact that it comes with a scheduler that means you can tell it to hoover daily, weekly or anything in between and it will duly do so at the day and hour you tell it then dutifully return to its charging station, plug itself in and get ready for the next time. At this point it was rapidly becoming no contest (where's my wallet?) But there is of course a down side. Said appliance only holds about a teacup of dust and has to be emptied (and cleaned) more or less after every use. But on the other hand, I was cleaning out the last one after every square metre so we're still quids in. It's also said that it doesn't hoover as well as you do. Well that of course depends a bit on who you are - and whether you are doing it at all. Obvious really. Something is generally better than nothing. So yet again the thumbs are up.

So that was it. Robot ordered, arrived, unpacked, charged and set going. Now you're dying to know if it's now stuck in the cupboard along with the exercise machine, 2 broken computers, 3 picnic sets and the miracle mop. Well, actually no. On first usage the boys and I sat with our feet up and mouths open while it was chugging round - happily enough, I imagine - doing what it does. And so it has continued, though by now we've managed to gather up our lower jaws and get on with other things while it beavers away. Yes it does occasionally leave bits we might have gone back to get and yes it does insist on trying to mate with the footstool but that apart, it's not half bad.

And the point is? Well actually besides encouraging laziness, there may be a real, eventual benefit. Apparently after sex and money, the thing couples argue most about is the sharing of domestic tasks. Now I doubt if home robots will help with problems one and two (just don't go there, please) but they might have unexpectedly good results on problem three. Not only does it do the job but the chances are that, being a technology thing, blokes are going to be much more interested (evidenced by the Cowan family blokes) and will willingly take over all hoover related tasks. From at least half the population's point of view this of course is a perfect outcome. And the sky's the limit. Robots that mow the lawn are already available and it's only a matter of time before they become more general purpose and can paint window frames, paper the hall and put up shelves. The only downside might be when public demand means they become available looking less like inflated wagon wheels (like our hoover) and more like Jane Asher or Kelly le Brock. Then, I guess we're back to square one...

Gloomy Times are Here Again

Alexander McCall Smith, popular author of the No. 1 Ladies Detective Agency series has some great book titles, one of which recently caught my eye. The Right Attitude to Rain is an Isabel Dalhousie novel involving McCall Smith's philosophical sleuth who spends off moments in between editing the Review of Applied Ethics solving crimes and dealing with other taxing human dilemmas. At this point I have no idea whether the book is much about rain, hail, snow or other inclement weather but it starting me thinking generally about unexpected nasties and how we put up with them.

Of course we have no shortage of raw material right now. Absolute acres (should that be hectares?) of broadcast and print space has been taken up over the past few months in reporting, analysing and commenting on what is variously called the "downturn", "recession" or "catastrophic meltdown" depending on how likely the speaker thinks they are to be blamed for it all. Numbers that only normally appear on astronomy charts have been turning up with pound and dollar signs attached, all percentage rates now seem to have a minus sign in front and Robert Peston, the BBC's Business Editor has had more time on TV than Anne Robinson herself. At this point of course the full implications have yet to show themselves but we are told to expect scarcer loans, negative equity, business failures, rising unemployment and eventually a hefty tax burden to be shared round with less enthusiasm than the Christmas night out bar bill. And while this may be the headline bad news, it goes along with all the stuff we know about already from ice caps to crime rates, inflation to hospital infections.

All pretty depressing stuff - and with Christmas coming up too! So is there anything to cheer the downcast soul? Anything to perk us up a bit just as the nights are fair drawing in and Seasonal Affective Disorder is doing its best to make us all feel terminally gloomy even regardless of the economic forecasts. Well, as ever, Loose Talk aims to bring a small ray of sunshine into the proceedings so here goes…

A good place to start might be the fact that we definitely still have it a darn sight better than most of our progenitors. If you ever did have the chance to "Meet the Ancestors" the first thing they might say would be "For goodness sake - what on earth are you moaning about?" (in Pictish). "You should try a diet of raw reindeer in a world where Pink Floyd aren't going to get together for another 50,000 years. How's that for depressing?" "True, true," we would then have to murmur, shamefacedly offering to leave an iPod with the said ancestor so they can appreciate the haunted mystic depths of Dark Side of the Moon which might be quite well suited to a neolithic lifestyle.

Then of course there are the millions in a worse condition. Just think about the untold hordes of failed X Factor applicants for starters. You think you're fed up? After putting your absolute all into a no holds barred hip hop version of I did it my Way, you have to collect your stuff and exit the building with the judges' final verdict ringing in your ears. "What part of 'no talent' are you struggling to understand". On the one hand we might think that anyone entering the car crash zone that reality TV has become has only their own self to blame but on the other hand what we see is a bunch of kids with real dreams and aspirations - realistic or not - dropped from a great height then jumped on purely for our collective amusement. Not really my idea of fun.

And if you're still feeling a bit depressed, there's the question of some other compensation that might take your mind off it all. For example, losing a job or 12 weeks pay might constitute a serious downturn in the personal economy for most of us. I don't imagine Mssrs. Ross and Brand are too much bothered for fairly obvious reasons. Point being, if you've got something else to cheer you up, bad news needn't be all that bad. And as they do say the best things in life are free. Remember Louis Armstrong singing so soulfully about "the bright blessed day, the dark sacred night." Unless you're one of the thousands who thought he was actually singing "The bride blessed the day, the dogs said goodnight" Look it up on www.kissthisguy.com the fantastic archive of misheard song lyrics for much innocent amusement and genuine cheering up. But misheard or not, the fact is the world is absolutely stuffed full of things to admire, respect, wonder at and stand in silence before. Soak it up man, as I would like to have said had I been born ten years earlier in time to be a genuine hippie.

Next up, you might be less depressed if what's going wrong in the world might not be what really matters to you. I remember our younger offspring coming up to our bedroom early one Saturday morning to tell us tearfully about the death of Princess Diana. "It's really, really sad," he sniffed, aged 6. "Lady Diana has died (more sniffing) and (floods of tears) they cancelled all the cartoons." So your shares are now worth a tenth of what they were six weeks ago. So nobody wants to buy your house and you can't get a mortgage for the new one. So business takings are down and you can't get a loan to develop new products. An hour spent in the company of Bugs Bunny and Co might be just what you need.

So, finally, what is the right attitude to rain and other inclement events? Apparently lines from the famous poem If are inscribed above the entrance to the Centre Court at Wimbledon. Rudyard encourages us to "meet with Triumph and Disaster, And treat those two impostors just the same…" No doubt this is a good idea but might be a bit beyond most of us. What I prefer is a nice bottle of Rioja, an evening in congenial company and the injunction to "Consider the lilies of the field…" (Matt. 6:28 etc). Check it out. Happy recession everyone.

It's good for the soul you know

- and it's traditional!

Around this time of year along with peace, goodwill and a double dose of Alka-Seltzer, it can be traditional to think about wrongs from the past we really ought to put right before another year goes by. In connection with which, it seems that the owner of an Indian food store in Bristol has recently received an apology letter and £100 from a former drug addict who stole cigarettes from the shop in 2001. The letter ran "Dear Sirs, I am writing this letter to make amends to you for something I have done in the past. About seven years ago I was walking past your shop late one night when I noticed that someone had broken into it. I used this opportunity to enter your shop where I stole 400 cigarettes … As part of my ongoing recovery I try to put right all of the wrongs I have done in the past, at least where I can, and this is why I am giving you back the money which I stole from you." Mr. Ahmed, owner of the shop said the thief's change of heart was "really good" and he intends to give the money to a drugs' charity.

Well, in the same spirit and in the hope of aiding my own recovery (I'll leave you to wonder from what) I would like to take this opportunity to confess, own up, make a clean break and hope the offended parties can accept this guilty plea. By the way, if you've already heard this story from the other side, Loose Talk would be grateful if you could pass on my apologies and £100.

Ok, here we go…more than twenty years ago (the further back the offence the more noble the confession) the young newlywed Cowans decided to pull their life savings, break open the piggy bank, take back all empty lemonade bottles and book a Valentine's Night out. Asking around for a nice restaurant we hadn't been to before, a friend casually asked "Have you tried The Forge? I think it's quite good," and gave us the number. Now, alarms bells should have rung had we paused to consider that said friend had something of a - shall we say "careful" attitude with money. So much so that at the Christmas just past she had admitted to buying a Christmas cake gift for her neighbour, cutting it in two and keeping half. So we should have been on our guard! Anyway, I duly phoned up and asked if we could book a table.

Second alarm bell should have followed the pause and rather puzzled acceptance at the other end of the line. Why might they have been reluctant to take our custom? Had they heard about the unfortunate incident with the Welsh rarebit, two live gerbils and a rubber band? Surely not. Palms were greased and we were fairly sure it was all covered up. Anyway our booking was accepted and I was left with that warm, snug, man-of-the-world feeling blokes enjoy having finally got their act together with Valentine's Day only hours away.

The night arrived. The Cowans got scrubbed up, dolled up and keyed up and off they went. The final alarm bell should have rung on arrival. This time it really did. The Forge was located in - how shall I put it - somewhat modest premises just across the road from the bus station. Drivers, ticket collectors (when they still existed in the wild), mechanics and office staff seemed to be wandering in and out in a steady stream still in their working clothes whether nice neat uniforms or oily boiler suits. Didn't they have a dress code?!? This was beginning to look a bit worrying. Doing the decent thing I left my life's companion in the car and went to investigate. Oh dear. One look was enough. It was the bus station transport caf'. Formica tables and grubby plastic chairs were occupied by employees of Walter Alexander's Bluebird Coaches happily wrapping their gnashers round bacon rolls. A sandwich counter, chocolate display and a fag machine were next the till. I think the juke box was playing King of the Road.

Ok - so we made a mistake. C'est la vie. If that had been it, it might have made a funny story and that's all. But it was worse. Much worse. The staff of the Forge, once they had gotten over the shock, had clearly taken our booking absolutely seriously and determined to make it an evening of magic and romance. Maybe they thought it was the final flowering of love between Big Ron from maintenance and Senga the wages clerk who both seemed to have both been working there since the days of horse drawn cabs. Or maybe it was Eric the Ticket Inspector's way of making things up to Connie the Clippie for finding three old age pensioners and a dog ticketless on last Thursday's high speed route from Carron Iron Works to Skinflats and fining her accordingly. Anyway, in the furthest corner, as far as possible from the blue haze of fag smoke and the sound of munching jaws was a small, secluded table. On it was a table cloth. A single red rose adorned the setting. A lemon yellow cotton screen was half way round the table.

Gulp. It was horrible. That's to say it was beautiful and made me feel horrible. Up to that point it was an honest mistake. We should never have asked the office skinflint to recommend a restaurant. The girl on the phone ought to have explained. I ought to have made an advance reconnoitre, found out what was what and phoned up to apologise and cancel. None of these things happened. So now here I was staring hideous embarrassment straight in the face. What to do? Wander casually past the wondering stares of the usual clientele and become fascinating fact of the week in all tea break chat ("Did you hear about that bloke that thought the Forge was a proper restaurant and booked a table?" "You're joking! Really?") or turn tail and leave the staff feeling like the victims of a prank that wasn't the least bit funny.

You guessed it and hence the reason for this grovelling apology. I went back to the car, mumbled an explanation and we shot off in the direction of Linlithgow where there are no bus stations. The only place we could find turned out be one of Scotland's top steak restaurants where we could only afford a glass of fruit juice, cheapest main course and a tangerine to finish. Served us right.

So, there you are. Confessed. And why at this time of year? If you prise away the wrapping paper, Christmas is really about redemption, reconciliation and forgiveness. And if you feel the need to share your confession with another human being, Loose Talk is listening… Happy Christmas.

Just keep swimming, just keep swimming ...

New Year resolutions. Don't you just hate them? After February 11th last year - and January 28th the year before - you've sworn never to make another one. Every diet you've ever been on has failed - including the last one that suggested using smaller plates. Every attempt to tighten up those tummy muscles and get a wee bit fitter has foundered by early February when, as all Fitness Suite professionals know, the rush has passed and fitness faddies go back to the armchair from whence they came. Even selfless efforts to be kinder to our fellow labourers in pay-off-the-mortgage-before-I'm-95-dom are doomed to failure as Senga tips a beaker of steaming chicken noodle cup-a-soup with croutons over your keyboard (and fingers) just as you're finishing the report on which your life depends. It all seems so pointless and predictable. New Year's resolutions are like the returning salmon of life, battling upstream against a relentless torrent of laziness, inertia, indolence and Match of the Day. Guess who wins?

And yet, and yet… some salmon must make it back or there could never be any little salmonettes (should that be salmonellas?) to head downstream to the Sargasso Sea - or wherever salmon go for a romantic break - to produce yet more teenage salmon studs who make it back against all odds - etc. etc. And there's the rub. Even though it seems a bit unlikely that John West's best are in fact our distant cousins, salmon nature and human nature share at least this in common - the triumph of hope over expectation. That's to say, when all we're left with is empties and a half full tub of turkey curry and the bin men have carted off the rest of the evidence, there is something about this time of year that almost demands at least an attempt at new beginnings. Our very determination never to make another resolution this side of an obituary in the Times seems to be having a little giggle at our expense. The sap is starting to stir and human nature longs to rise with it. Thoughts of how pointless it all is are put to one side and despite it all we really feel we ought to have another go. Just this once…

But what to resolve? It has to be something substantial so deciding not to step on the cracks like Christopher Robin doesn't quite cut it. Now, if you were determined not to step on the chewing gum - that might be more of a challenge. It also has to be something aimed at local if not universal betterment so giving even less to charity and being ruder to other road users also fail to qualify. Shame on you for thinking it. In fact, to be honest, (I know this is really against the grain) it even has to be something that stands a fighting chance of succeeding. So you can toss out the Orkney's Strongest Man application form right now.

But what should it be? Actually, you may consider this cheating but I'd like to cast my modest vote in favour of something all of us desperately need, that makes a real difference and stands an even better chance than John Sergeant of getting through to the dance off. It's persistence. Just keeping on going when everything in you feels like giving up. Pure and simple. Keeping relentlessly plodding on might not be considered very sexy nowadays by go-getters and high fliers, but it really is what makes the world go round. Forget Burt Bacharach, The Band and Doris Day, all awarded lifetime Grammies in 2008. Who should get the real lifetime achievement awards? Here are a few suggestions…

How about lone parents for starters? I cannot begin to imagine the courage, fortitude and sheer doggedness it takes to bring up kids on your own, without that special someone to snuggle up to and lovingly whisper "I am absolutely knackered - it's your turn now." Maybe it's even worse in teenage years when it might involve a bit less physical graft but bucket loads more mental energy. What happens when the little darling fails to appear after the school disco and you can't leave the younger one to go and look? What indeed. I have no idea. Now you might be thinking this doesn't totally fit the New Year's resolution job description since it's not exactly something you have much choice over - unlike giving up the fags or booking tickets for Tahiti. But doesn't that make it all the tougher? It just goes on and on and times you think you might be seeing light at the end of the tunnel are just as likely to be an approaching train.

My second nomination is inspired by one of this year's Christmas pressies. Someone in the family got (from me) a DVD entitled "Rikki and Me", the film of the stage show of the book of the life of Rikki Fulton by wife Kate. We remember Rikki with admiration, affection and sore sides for Francie and Josie, Rev. I. M. Jolly, Supercop and a host of other characters, sketches and generally great Scottish fun. Rikki was a comic genius and aided by Jack Milroy made two Glasgow teddy boys one of the icons of their generation. But less well known is that he suffered from Alzheimer's Disease in later life and was cared for by Kate until that became impossible and professional help was needed. For a man who loved words and had a talent for putting them together in the funniest combinations, it must have been hugely frustrating to find himself unable to speak coherently or remember the punch line of a gag. And how painful for those who loved and admired him to see him sinking into a bog of confusion and forgetfulness. But yet again, persistence is the name of game. Thousands of husbands, wives, even parents and children have to do that every day of the year - and New Year makes very little difference to it.

Of course there are dozens of causes and millions of individuals besides these who take a deep breath and plunge on into another year just hoping to keep their collective chins up in the face of discouragement and despair. Bankers longing for sympathy. That girl from Belarus that keeps emailing me looking for "good husband in the west". Even Falkirk Bairns' supporters. Anyway, Happy New Year to all of you (better late than never) and in the words of Dory, Marlin's pal from Finding Nemo, "Just keep swimming, just keep swimming…"

And to my eldest son Rupert I leave...

The Laughing Policeman & Walk Like an Egyptian

Alongside all the soap suds, celebrity worship and so called "reality" we stump up our licence fees for, something genuinely entertaining and thought provoking occasionally pops up on our wonderful BBC. Such an item is the "Inheritance Tracks" slot on Saturday Live (Radio 4 - Sat mornings). The idea of a rich relation leaving you an unexpected bonus is entertaining and thought provoking enough but, let's face it, is neither going to last a lifetime nor make much a difference to who and what you are. Likewise the meagre contents of the Post Office Savings Account you hope to pass on to your own little darlings.

Inheritance tracks, on the other hand, asks well-ish known people to think about the musical inheritance they've received from a previous generation and what they want to pass on to someone else. It's fascinating. Choices are often unexpected, sometimes intriguing and always worth listening to. For example:

- Model and fashion icon Twiggy chose The Laughing Policeman by Charles Penrose and Yesterday by The Beatles
- TV host Jerry Springer chose Tennessee Waltz by Patti Page & Coat Of Many Colours by Dolly Parton
- Earl Spencer chose Ernie The Fastest Milkman In The West by Benny Hill and The Living Years by Mike and the Mechanics.
- Brian Eno chose a piano roll version of Jerusalem and Peace Be Still by Rev James Cleveland and the Angelic Choir.

While I am (of course) a Desert Island Discs fan, the selections stars choose to take to their imaginary tropical paradise are basically the tunes they think they could stand to hear repeatedly for the forty years it might take to whittle a scale model of the Hamnavoe to bring them back to civilisation. This is something more. It's about how you got to be who you are and what you want to pass on of yourself to someone else - within the limits of a 3 minutes 50 second song.

Sadly, I grew up in a musically deprived environment. My Dad's favourite albums were the Best of Jim Reeves and Country Gospel Singalong. Nuff said. My Mum, while she did play the piano, never got beyond Redemption Hymns and Singspiration. On the other hand, my elder brother - almost ten years older - did bring home South Pacific (Some Enchanted Evening, Bali Ha'i and Nothing Like a Dame), the Best of the Dubliners and most of Fairport Convention - unfortunately not in person. Maybe not Sergeant Pepper but certainly an improvement. In due course middle brother produced The Incredible String Band - weird - and Tubular Bells - even weirder. I can vividly remember us all sitting round with our mouths hanging open listening to the now unmistakable opening bars - ting ting - ting ting - that just seemed to keep on going - and going - and going. By this time the album had already become iconic however not being a very avant garde household (we thought coffee was a bit newfangled) we had no idea what to expect and asked ourselves "Is that it?" before putting Jim Reeves back on. I know better now.

When eldest brother got engaged however and brought his new fiancée home things really began to look up. The Moody Blues Days of Future Passed was followed by Threshold of a Dream and In Search of the Lost Chord. I was hooked. (Apparently Prog is now becoming cool again so I can mention this in a family column without being lynched.) Then Neil Young's After the Gold Rush and Harvest. Great. Cat Stevens. Vaughan Williams. Pentangle. I could go on. Music I still listen to and love. What an inheritance. As the poet put it "Bliss was it in that dawn to be alive, But to be young was very heaven!"

However, the rules of this game also involve thinking what you might now pass on and that's a little harder. Over the years I've put together a number of father and son weekends, usually centred round a musical event. Since I'm paying, these do not involve Hot Chip, Daft Punk or Green Day. I probably couldn't afford the tickets. Instead we've done Yes's 30th Anniversary tour (they looked like it might be the 300th and eldest son was the youngest person there by about 30 years), Jeff Wayne's War of the Worlds (featuring Jeff himself, the real Justin Hayward and a pretend Richard Burton) and, best of all, the Aussie Pink Floyd Show. Whether any of these will stick and become my own kids' inheritance tracks only time will tell, but a good time was had by all.

But that's not entirely the point. I certainly feel I will not have failed utterly as a father if my sons can go through life whistling the 5/4 intro to Money and the melody line of Eve of the War. But, good as that is, there's a bit of me that feels it probably isn't enough.

Sometimes you hear parents saying "We don't tell them what to believe - we just let them make up their own minds", and on the face of it this sounds quite reasonable. None of us want to impose our own beliefs without young people thinking it out for themselves. The problem is that leaving kids free from our own highly flawed and biased guidance does not put life decision making on a level playing field. Every day a million messages are pumped out to young people from sources not nearly as even handed as you might want to be. This is what's cool. This is what everybody does. This is what you have a right to enjoy and this is what you can't be without - because you're worth it. It's make up and fashion, music and gadgets, sexuality and glamour, alcohol and other substances even more intoxicating. Sometimes you feel even The Laughing Policeman isn't quite going to give them what they need.

So what do I want to pass on to my kids? Beatles, Kinks and Floyd may be a good start but I hope that's not all they say they've got when they appear on Inheritance Tracks 2050.

Not just stuff - stuff with a tale to tell

Futurology is a tricky business. Sometimes those paid to pontificate on what future years might hold get it reasonably right - but more often spectacularly wrong. For example it didn't take rocket science to predict the crisis in care we're now experiencing with longer lifespans and insufficient resources. Now we're seeing the consequences. And by the way, why is rocket science the standard of brilliance everything is compared to? Apparently lots of the brightest and best from Los Alamos found their way into guess where - banking! So from now on we'll be saying "after all, it isn't goldfish breeding!" Evidence may come to suggest that goldfish breeders, while a bit less showy, are just as bright and have done us all a lot less harm.

However, that aside, the more interesting social trends are often the ones absolutely nobody saw coming. Who would have guessed that ABBA would now be cool again or that your house would be worth less than you paid for it in 1963. Hold on to that Bay City Rollers memorabilia - you never know. My interesting social trend of the week however is neither of these. It's something you'd have thought an increasingly affluent society wouldn't have any time for and we'd all keep quiet about even if we did indulge. It's second hand stuff - and it's great.

Ebay has become an internet monster and apparently we all now love it and brag about it. See this pair of thigh high boots, lava lamp and complete set of Thunderbird toys. All off Ebay. £1.17 plus postage. Not bad! It seems nowadays that people are furnishing their entire houses - maybe even buying houses - off Ebay. Though surely the postage on a complete house must be prohibitive. But the point is that almost anything you want, lots of things you've never even heard of and even items you thought were certainly immoral and possibly illegal - someone, somewhere has them, no longer wants them and is willing to ship them to you for a pittance. And what are we buying? Clothes of course - especially kids stuff, toys, CDs and records (what is now apparently called "vinyl"), car bits (we bought a replacement door for £10), mobile phones and chargers, computers, sports gear, office equipment - you name it. In fact this very evening a friend was telling me about his extensive snorkel collection - all off Ebay. I kid you not. Fifteen. Don't ask.

It reminds me of the story of a university campus trying to introduce email before the days of the wonderful Internet. Nobody understood it, wanted it or used it - until they introduced a For Sale and Wanted service. Then it was inundated. Because everybody likes the idea of making some cash out of stuff that's been cluttering up the attic of their last three houses. And that same everybody loves a bargain - especially if what you want can be obtained in no other legal way. So Ebay is simply the three in one that lubricates the deal connecting the haves and the have nots aided by a modest transfer of cash.

Now that undoubtedly is great, particularly in our new credit crunched world - but there is something more. Something I like even better than either liberating floor space or easing the burden on the wallet. It's this. What you buy second hand has a history. It's been somewhere else living a different life before you got your hands on it. And sometimes it has a tale to tell.

Take this example. I've recently been reading the excellent Anne Lamott - specifically Bird by Bird and Travelling Mercies - which I got second hand off Amazon. Just by chance - is there such a thing? - I happened to look in the inside front cover of Bird by Bird (which by the way is a book on writing not ornithology). There it was, in plain black ballpoint, a simple message. Morgan, Never stop writing, never stop loving! Enjoy and be good! Kathryn. You can see where I'm going with this. Who's Morgan and who's Kathryn? And what was - or is - their relationship? Were they husband and wife or friends or work colleagues or fellow members of a writing group or people who met on a bus and started talking and realised they both loved writing. What was the occasion of the gift? Was it a birthday or Christmas or just as a pick-me-up? Maybe it was given to celebrate the publication of Morgan's first novel by his editor or his old English teacher. And why did he get rid of it to the Internet bookseller who sold it to me? Maybe he had decided he was never going to get published and so had given up writing? How would Kathryn feel if she knew Morgan had sold her gift? Maybe Morgan couldn't write through his long final illness and the book was eventually sold along with his shoes, overcoat and typewriter.

An inscription in a flyleaf is perhaps a particularly poignant illustration of the earlier life of second hand stuff but it's not the only one that comes to mind. About ten cars ago our vintage vehicle of the time was getting an unusually thorough clean when bingo - a plain gold wedding band turned up in a crevice under the back seats. It was (and is) inscribed simply W S M - M N 19/1/19. Naturally we tried to trace previous owners of the car and even put an advert in the Sunday Post but all to no avail. So we still have it. I'm holding it right now. You could easily let you imagination loose on that one. It was just after the First World War. She thought she would lose him but he came home safely. They married and had their family. Perhaps the eldest daughter got the ring for her wedding then maybe granddaughter got it for hers. One day they went for a drive and a picnic with friends and came home without the ring. They searched everywhere - house, road, even the park where they ate their sandwiches but ring there was none.

So second hand is great in all sorts of ways, but I think it's not fair just to say it's stuff nobody wants any more. I prefer the thought behind an alternative website to Ebay - www.preloved.co.uk. So, Morgan, if you're out there, I hope you're still writing and loving. And offspring of W S M - get in touch. It would be nice to see the story complete.

How weird are you - really?

We've been told the 60s marked the end of all the old conformities and the start of an exciting new age of freedom. Suddenly we could wave bye bye to the drabness, greyness and compliance of the 50s and say hullo to a brave new world of individuality, self expression and uniqueness. How exciting.

When I say "all" of course, there were always going to be exceptions. What went down a storm in Carnaby St. may not have been quite such a hit on the High Street in Brechin. And Mums across the land still seemed to have something against purple shirts, suede jackets, Chelsea boots and kaftans. I can vouch for this from painful experience, bearing in mind the months of wheedling, nagging, cajoling and, let's face it, downright begging, that finally got me to Dillon's the Gent's Outfitters for a shirt that wasn't white bri-nylon or grey flannel!

Bri-nylon - if you remember - was an exciting new fabric invented in a physics lab in the sixties that did a pretty good job if you didn't have a Van de Graaff generator handy and needed to demonstrate 3000 volts. Pulling it over your head sounded like a bad signal from Radio Luxembourg and you could come home from school to find thread, string, bits of old tissue paper and sometimes even small children mysteriously attached. Grey flannel on the other hand was just boring and itchy. It made you seem like a boring, itchy person. Which is exactly what you were. Once in the shop, I tried begging a bit more for the orange corduroy one with a button down collar and tailored fit but eventually thought myself lucky to get a cotton one in Conservative Blue.

So not surprisingly most of us were definitely up for a bit less conformity and a bit more fun and that's what the 60s and subsequent decades were supported to offer. Which made it intriguing to hear a bit on the news this week. Apparently anti globalisation protesters and climate change campaigners (shouldn't they be anti-climate change campaigners) have been planning to invade the City of London prior to the G20 talks and targeting bankers for special attention. Clearly this is not a good thing in terms of law and order but the intriguing bit is how security is to be stepped up. Besides a few extra big burly blokes loitering in the foyer and the locking of non essential doors (after the horse has bolted some might say), City bankers are being advised not to dress so much like bankers but try to look a bit more like normal people. Clearly there is something that environmental campaigners and anarchists can recognise at 50 paces that says banker in unmistakable terms. In other words, a bankery "look".

It seems that even after forty years of growing self expression and diversity there is something in human nature that just craves the sense of belonging and acceptance you get from just being like everyone else. And that applies to bankers as much as goths, punks, hippies and chavs. Think of the group photos that usually mark the conclusion of all G7 / G20 or G99 events. All 7, 20 or 99 Prime Ministers (or equivalent) form up on the steps and smile for the cameras. Every single one of them (except for Angela Merkel) dressed in dark suits, white shirts, bright (but not garish) ties and polished black shoes. It almost makes you hope the shirts are bri-nylon and are going to erupt in a shower of blue sparks. It's the Prime Ministerial uniform. Probably quite like the City banker uniform. And that's the point. Whether it's Armani suits or pierced eyebrows everyone likes to belong.

So, in spite everything we say about the freedom to be yourself, I wonder if we are every bit as conformist as our parents, it's just that the number of different uniforms available may have increased a bit.

Which makes me think about how we might all really behave if it weren't for the pressure to conform. It was Macaulay (apparently) who said "The essence of a man's character is what he would do if he knew he would never be found out". Setting aside the actually illegal and immoral (both of which go on anyway regardless of what anybody thinks), what would you like to do that you feel the pressure to confirm currently renders impossible? Change your dress sense? Your name? Your occupation? Your hobbies? Maybe your whole identity?

Jenny Joseph's great poem "Warning" tells about what she plans to do when she's old and doesn't care any more. Instead of "paying the rent, not swearing in the street and setting a good example for the children" she says she'll:

*"sit down on the pavement when I'm tired / and
gobble up samples in shops / and press alarm
bells /and run with my stick along public railings /
and make up for the sobriety of my youth"*

I remember a visit some years ago to what I still think of as the capital
of weirdness, Venice Beach in California. As a generally shy, well
behaved, Scottish youth I found myself wandering around jaw on the
deck at what seemed like life from other planets. Some bloke who
seemed to lack the gene for self preservation was juggling with running
chain saws. An old guy who looked like he'd have difficulty making it
to the day centre was tap dancing in roller skates. Sundry others were
exhibiting body art and piercings that made them look like Picasso
people brought to life. It was - weird. But who am I to complain? It
wasn't doing any harm, in fact quite the opposite. The place had a
carnival atmosphere. And as far as weirdness was concerned they still
had a way to go to catch up with the duck billed platypus or hammer
head shark.

So it can be done. Starting from the 60s we seem to have gotten the
notion that the sum total of human variation has increased. Maybe
we might be overplaying this a bit. And maybe if the bankers had
conformed a bit less to being like bankers and behaved a bit more like
goths and punks things might have been better all round.

Whose Blog is it anyway?

I was listening to a bit of news recently on some government crisis or other - there seem to be plenty to choose from - when the reporter happened to quote a comment from Old Labour stalwart John Prescott. Although not normally a Pressa fan my ears pricked up to hear this came not from an interview, a newspaper article, a speech to the TUC or even his latest book. It was from his blog site! I did an aural double take. John Prescott? Blog site? There musht be shum mishtake, offisher. Somehow or other I just couldn't think of Mr. Prescott - big beast of BB (Before Blair) Labour as he is - as a blogger. But it's true. I've been there and it does exist - even if it is embedded in a site devoted to achieving a fourth Labour term. And here we can read Prescott doings, musings and moaning to our hearts' content - if that sort of thing doesn't give you heartburn. Whether he actually sits up in bed uploading it himself at the end of a busy campaigning day or simply scribbles it down and passes to some more IT savvy functionaries we may never know. But blogger he is.

Now the odd thing about this is that firstly, had it been revealed 10 years ago that John Prescott was a blogger, we might merely have narrowed our eyes and muttered "I'm not surprised, I never trusted him anyway" without the faintest idea what a blogger was or whether it was even legal. In another 10 years it might be much more surprising to find out he isn't - since nowadays it looks like almost everybody is one or wants to be one.

Now, if you're one of the dwindling band that remain unblogged (sounds like something you do to a sink) and mystified as to the what, where, how and (most importantly) why of blogging, then put simply, it's a contraction of "Web logging" and consists of an online diary, online ramblings or whatever else you feel like saying - online. Once upon a time nobody gave a hoot what you thought about global warming, US foreign policy, children's footwear or what you had for breakfast. And that was fine because nobody had to listen to you droning on about it - or if they did, they had the option of going outside to watch paint dry as a better alternative. Now, while nobody still gives a hoot, the phenomenon of blogging means you can put your thoughts online for the whole world to read. Out of all the countless millions with nothing better to do than web surf when they should be working, somebody's bound to stumble across your pearls of wisdom and find themselves inspired. Suddenly all of the prejudices, misconceptions, trivia and amusing anecdotes the family have heard far too many times have a global audience. Bingo!

Well, despite what you might think about Loose Talk's craving for publicity, here I have to admit I have no blog. Nor a Facebook page. Nor a MySpace site. Nor a Twitter account. Nor an MSN presence. Which actually means I hardly exist at all. Firstly, I simply haven't the time to post a mixture of ramblings and ravings online, and secondly, anyone forced to listen to the live audio feed (what we used to call "talking") pretty soon wants it to stop so I worry that blogging might turn out a bit dispiriting if the same reaction is multiplied several million times. Whether I like it or not (or care or not) though, blogging is now a huge phenomenon. A figure I got from over a year ago quoted the number at 112.8 million blogs! So by now probably over 200 million people are publishing online when they ought to be doing their homework or mowing the lawn.

So what are we to make of it all? No doubt the whole idea of web "presence" seems like a pretty soft target for the majority of us over 40s. Indeed it might be tempting to see it in the way John Peel famously described Emerson, Lake and Palmer's performance at the Isle of Wight festival as "a tragic waste of electricity". Millions of kids worldwide are spending their evenings posting pictures and rude remarks on each other's Facebook pages instead of doing something more constructive - like their Higher Geography assignment due for Monday morning. Politicians keen to keep up with social trends are jumping on the bandwagon (Barak Obama has 6,239,289 supporters on Facebook - I couldn't find out how many John Prescott has). Terrible innit? Surely a total waste of time and bandwidth.

Not so fast though. Can you remember where you first heard the term "blog"? For millions it was in connection with the online postings of Salam Pax better known as the Bahgdad Blogger. Salam Pax (a pseudonym made up of Arabic and Latin words for "peace") told the world what was going on in Baghdad during and after the 2003 invasion. His blog became an essential source of news from neither an official Iraqi source nor a US Government point of view. So blogging simply lets anyone say pretty much what they want on any subject - irrespective of what the Government or the neighbours think. Of course 99% of it will be trivial twaddle but so what? The same could easily be said of much of what appears in print. Today's newspapers are tomorrow's chip wrappers, as they say. At least blogging doesn't involve hacking down swathes of forest to print it all. And it isn't controlled by Rupert Murdoch. So even if I have absolutely no interest in what multitudes of teenage kids have to say to one another, multitudes of other teenagers certainly do and is it any of my business anyway?

Voltaire, the French philosopher, is quoted as saying "I disapprove of what you say, but I will defend to the death your right to say it." Nowadays we could substitute "blog" for "say". And yes - sadly, this even applies to Mr. Prescott. As long as we still retain the freedom not to have to read it.

Nostalgia: it just ain't what it used to be

I was recently watching some fascinating old footage of Scottish life in the 50s and 60s. It was all trams, paddle steamers, horse drawn carts and short trousered kids playing keepie uppie in the street. The film was great and full of detail about things that largely don't exist any more - though trams are due for a come back as you'll know if you've been stuck in road works in the middle of Edinburgh recently. What struck me more though was the interviews with people of that generation talking about their lives. The social changes they have lived through can hardly be overstated but their nostalgia seemed to be not only for jeely pieces and the Palais but for a world that was essentially more familiar and understandable. The contrast to what we're living through right now hardly needs to be stated. It's not just a case of what things are changed but more the pace of change in general.

Anyway, that set me thinking about what sorts of things are changing right now that might put all talk of bare feet, party lines and Sunday School trips in the shade. If a similar film were to be made (and uploaded to Youtube) in a few years time, what will we be talking about that's making life different through the present generation? Futurology is a highly hazardous venture of course - according to anyone in the 60s we should all now be served by robots, munching our way through a dinner of nutrition pills and dressed in bacofoil. Having done the risk assessments though perhaps a modest venture might be possible. If you're willing to fasten your safety belts and adopt the brace position here are a couple of Loose Talk suggestions.

Technology has to be an obvious place to start. A survey on the Today programme this very morning stated that 80% of us now view broadband as essential on a par with electricity and water. Ten years ago we would all have been asking "Broadband - is that something for holding your trousers up?" Now we all know what it is and we need it. In fact I have to concur with this having lost email contact with the universe for a whole FOUR days last week. I was electronically incommunicado. A digital non person. Nobody could speak to me and likewise I to them. Was it just my customary reticence and shy demeanour or had I taken offence at everyone? Neither. I wanted to talk but CompuServe wouldn't let me. I have a somewhat older friend who now admits to having got an email address at last - but keeps it firmly down at the library. I have some sympathy. If it could all just be held at arms length it might not be so frightening, challenging and intrusive.

And that takes us to random suggestion number two. One effect of technology has been an explosion in choice - dozens (if not hundreds) of TV channels, Internet streaming of every sort and even an explosion in conventional print. Ok - that's what we have more of, but I think there's also something we've got less of. When I was at school (and maybe when you were too) everyone watched the Morecambe and Wise Christmas Specials - and talked about it next day. Well, when I say "everyone", actually it was a mere 26 million - about half the UK population, but for all practical purposes that's as near as makes no difference. Now, the more choices we have, the less we have in common. The thought that half the population would share almost anything now seems a thing of the past. This was brought home recently by my own little bit of nostalgic self indulgence. I finally managed to get my paws on a DVD set of a great mini series about the Apollo Programme narrated by the equally great Tom Hanks. Granted this isn't everybody's cup of freeze dried nutritional supplement but it reminded me of the worldwide phenomenon that was the first moon landing. We all stayed up till 3.00am to watch it and I had the front page from next morning's Daily Express up on my bedroom wall for three years afterwards. Even if you're not the least bit interested in that sort of thing now - back in 1969 everybody was. It gave us a sense of common humanity and shared experience - maybe something we could do with a little bit more of right now. Incidentally - did you know you can now buy a Haynes Owners Workshop Manual to the Apollo 11 Lunar Excursion Module for a mere £12.59 from Amazon. Getting a LEM to actually work on might be trickier.

Finally from the sublime to the pure dead brilliant - Oor Wullie - a great Scottish icon if ever there was one. Whatever scrapes Wullie might get into, everything works out fine in the final frame as he sits happily on his bucket with a plate of Maw's mince and tatties to look forward to. I, as I write, have next to me a glass of not bad Spanish red wine and will shortly be enjoying spaghetti bolognese. Not terribly exotic I grant you but both largely unknown when I was Wullie's age. The nearest we got to exotic was macaroni cheese or sweet corn. More normal fare was corned beef, potted haugh, tripe, tongue, liver and cod roe - all largely unknown to youngsters today. They, by contrast, enjoy pizza (the first one I tasted was deep fried), fajitas, paninis, paella, sweet and sour, chicken tikka masala and cookie dough ice cream. Whether today's diet is better or worse seems something of a curate's egg (if you'll let me away with that one) but it is undoubtedly different - and signals an increasingly diverse global lifestyle. What a change.

So what will we be doing when the interviewer calls on Skype in a few years time to get our reminiscences about the past? Maybe enjoying chicken in black bean sauce while watching a DVD of the best of Morecambe and Wise and feeling nostalgic about 2009. Ah - it just ain't what it used to be.

What's on Your Bucket List?

Jack Nicholson is a billionaire health care tycoon. The mantra that keeps costs down and makes him so successful is "two to a room - no exceptions." Unfortunately when he contracts cancer and finds himself a patient in his own hospital ward the same rule still applies. Morgan Freeman is a garage mechanic though he always wanted to be a history professor. When he gets a cancer diagnosis he ends up in the same hospital - in the same room. Like the man said "two to a room - no exceptions."

Despite their differences - and after a shaky start - the two men begin to hit it off and start sharing about their lives and aspirations. One day Nicolson spots Freeman writing something and picks up the discarded page. It's what Freeman calls his Bucket List - all the things he wants to do before he kicks the bucket. Neither of them may have much time left but at least Nicolson has the money to make it happen. He offers to finance the trip and together they define their joint list and head off on a journey as much of self discovery as completion of any of their lifetime goals.

Such is the plot of "The Bucket List", a movie we recently watched on DVD having given in to the adverts and signed up to Lovefilm.com. The story is engaging and the performances convincing but it's the concept of the list itself that surely makes you think. We are so often caught up with the practicalities of life - paying the bills, ferrying the kids about, passing exams, applying for jobs, mowing the lawn, doing what we have to do - that we rarely stop to think about the big picture. What do we really want to accomplish? What are our life ambitions and what are we doing about achieving them? Of course we want our kids to be happy and we want long lasting stable relationships for ourselves. We want to do well at work and have enough money to enjoy the odd special treat. We want to pay attention to spiritual realities and not just this passing material world. We want to offend as few as possible and to have an overall positive impact. All well and good and worthy enough but that's pretty common to all of us. What do you want to do? What would be on your list?

120

The list Nicolson and Freeman's characters come up isn't a bad place to start. It has a few of the "go there - do that" types of things but also a few that lift it to a slightly higher level such as Witness something truly majestic, Help a complete stranger for a common good, Laugh till I cry and Drive a Shelby Mustang. As the story progresses however we see that it is one of the least exciting items on the list - Get back in touch that has some unforeseen implications. Eventually the message of the film seems to be that it's in being in touch with others that we find more of the significance of life than in merely visiting Stonehenge or the Great Wall of China. Freeman's marriage revives before the cancer finally wins out and Nicolson gets back in touch with his estranged daughter. At Freeman's funeral he reveals how much their relationship has meant to him - despite their differences in taste, status and life experience.

So you get the idea - and we've been skirting round it for too long already. What's on your bucket list? A former colleague once shared with me the wise words "Nobody on their deathbed says 'I wish I'd spent more time at the office'". But what do they say - apart from "Kiss me Hardy." What have you always wanted to do or be or experience that you're in danger of never fulfilling unless you seriously get your ass into gear and do something about it? Even if some of them might seem a bit unlikely right now - you never know what opportunities may come your way. If you aim at nothing (the business gurus tell us) that's what you're certain of hitting.

So you're wanting to know what's on my list (not that I'm crass enough to actually have a list you understand). Well there's a bit of travel as you'd expect - Spain I have managed - Israel I would like to -if it ever calms down. Also some new skills to master and the saxophone is definitely coming along - don't let the neighbours tell you otherwise. As regards experiences, however, this summer was beginning to look like a bit of a disappointment. I've always fancied seeing a Space Shuttle launch however the entire programme comes to an end next year so this might have been my last chance. With the loving understanding of my fellow travellers I got all the Florida brochures, checked the NASA website and even registered with a houseswap web site (anyone want a fortnight in Finstown for two weeks in Florida?) but somehow couldn't quite get my act together to get it all booked up. Which has turned out to be a pretty good thing actually. Instead we're planning to fulfill another goal we never thought possible. In early August (final health checks permitting) we'll be leaving for a year in New Zealand for a mixture of a grown up gap year and a revival of student life. Never fear though, along with clothes, computers and a saxophone the entire Loose Talk office is also being packed up, loaded into a series of extra large containers and shipped lock, stock and beer barrel out to join us.

So for a year or so there is a possibility that I might be sounding less middle aged, less grumpy and less like Victor Meldrew on a bad day. And if, in the process of getting the house ready to let, cleaning out all drawers and cupboards and storing our possessions I happen to find my mobile phone charger - well that'll be another life ambition to cross off the list.

So what is on your list? Are there some connections you need to revive or some potential as yet unfulfilled? Think about it. And if you need someone to talk it over with Loose Talk is at your service. Drop us a line at "Life Longings Fulfilled, c/o Loose Talk, Finstown, Orkney". And don't forget to include a stamped addressed envelope.

Back to School

Just three little words but what a reaction! Mums and Dads across the land are going "Yes! We've made it through another summer. Normal service can be resumed. And I don't care if it does cost me a new pair of trainers or a pocket money raise." Kids are meanwhile going "Noooooooooo! It seemed so long. Now it's all gone. And I haven't got my geography homework done or read A Tale of Two Cities. It's so unfair. Wonder if I can get a new pair or trainers or a pocket money raise?"

Both are of course entirely right to feel this way. How could it be otherwise? When the bell rang for the end of the last period of the last day of the last week of summer term, from the under 16s point of view, six weeks might as well be six months or six years. They basically stretch out for as far as the imagination can reach - longer than Cliff 's "Complete Hits Collection" or the time it takes a teenager to clean their room. Parents likewise think it could also last forever but view the prospect with somewhat less enthusiasm.

Then suddenly it's over. Just a few minutes after they were bawling "School's Out" the end of term disco, it's "School's Back In" and here we go again. Incidentally, given that Alice Cooper was 60 last year, don't you think it's about time he produced a classic rock anthem for parents overjoyed to have survived six weeks and got rid of the little darlings for another year?

Well, having coped with both School's Out and Back to School experiences a total of 15 times, this year it's working out a wee bit differently. With older son left school a couple of years now and younger one liberated this summer, in a moment of madness we've decided to prolong the agony by going back to school ourselves. Specifically, these musings come to you from EastWest College of Intercultural Studies, Gordonton, nr. Hamilton, North Island , New Zealand. Yes, I know Intercultural Studies sounds like something dreamed up by an academic Dean keen for the grants but having run of real things to study (like Introduction to Tolkein, Advanced Lennon and McCartney and 3D Raffia Work) however I assure you it is a real subject – of a sort. Have a look at www.eastwest.ac.nz if you're curious.

So – just in case you're fooled into taking the Lifelong Learning mantra seriously - I thought I should warn you what it's really like. First, you are likely to be mixing with teenagers all over again – just when you thought you'd dumped them off at uni or gap years and the coast was clear. Actually, there's a surprisingly wide age span here, from those even older than us (surprising but true) to those who look as if they just finished a paper round the week before. But – let's face it – that has to be kind of refreshing. Teenagers maybe, but at the same time, teenagers for whom WE HAVE NO RESPONSIBILITY – whoa!! In fact we went and heard two of them playing at Hamilton's Audio Café venue at the weekend just to show our "not as boring as you think" credentials and weren't deafened. Nice.

Secondly, since we've been so perverse as to do the grown up gap year thing so far from home, we're having to explain where Orkney is all over again – just when we'd got used to the combined effect of child care scandals and BB making us think we should be known throughout the galaxy. Even when people have heard the name, the majority opinion is either somewhere off the west coast or quite close to Iceland. In one case, a nice lady assured me she and her husband had actually been there (or "here" depending on your point of view). Wow, she said, the quality of your cattle! We're from farming folk but we've never seen anything like that. And so near the North Pole too... I took the compliment and didn't argue.

Next up there's the small matter of assignments. At our time of life we're kind of out of the way of being delighted with 18 out of 20 or being asked to memorise and label a map of the Middle East. (True, I tell you, all true.) However, in our favour, we're not texting like mad at the back of the class, caught up in unrequited love (which can take up some time and effort) or turning up for lectures late because we were down the pub till chucking out time then round at a mate's till waking up time and still on the bus at starting time. By the way, on the subject of lectures, I got some advice from son number one. "Whatever you do Dad," (he told me, all serious) "don't ask questions. We have adults in our lectures that ask questions. Everybody hates it. All we want to do is get out and go home and they keep on asking stuff as if they were actually interested!" I can understand how irritating that must be but sometimes I just can't help myself. Is it my fault I'm here because I actually am interested?

So lots of things are different – like not taking my laundry home and doing my assignments on computer for instance. Some are the same. Hours in the library and always having a set of deadlines hanging over you. On the other hand we get 10 weeks off over what they call summer and civilised people call Christmas. However, whatever you call it, I just hope they have an end of term disco when they put "Schools Out" on to finish with. I think I might enjoy that.

Stand Back – it's Listomania!

I was recently wandering a bit aimlessly round our local bookshop in downtown Hamilton (New Zealand not Lanarkshire – we're spending a year out here studying) when I happened to notice alongside piles of landscape photography hardbacks and rugby biographies something a little more interesting. It was the intriguingly entitled "1,000 Recordings to Hear before you Die: A Listener's Life List" by Tom Moon, subtitled "The More you Love Music, the More Music you Love". A moment's hesitation, a brief flick through, then the key factor – it was half price – and off to the tills. I have to admit though, even had it been full price, I might still have parted with my shekels.

It's fascinating and I've been dipping in and out for the past 3 weeks. The format is fairly straightforward. It's alphabetical from ABBA (not AC/DC though they do get in there) right through to ZZ Top (likewise Frank Zappa) with about a dozen different indexes plus a further section of also rans that didn't quite make the top 1000. Entries are necessarily brief or we'd end up with something bigger than Young's Analytical Concordance to the Bible, and consist of about a page each, sometimes a photo but not always and a few hundred words about why that particular recording is so great. Each entry ends with some categorisation, key tracks, next choices and where to go next if you like it so far.

So why the fascination? Isn't this up to about 9.5 on the geek-o-meter? Well probably – but so what. The first time through, the main thing was "Do they like the same stuff I like and for the same reasons?" No worries there mate - as everybody here says all the time. There's Exodus from Bob Marley, Pet Sounds from the Beach Boys, Miles Davies Kind of Blue, Joni Mitchell's Court and Spark and John Martyn's Solid Air – though Yes only get into the also rans. Great. But that's a bit like spending an evening at a gourmet chocolate tasting and feeding your face till you're sick at the very first stall. The thing is to browse along, try a little bit of everything, see what might be tasty and nibble a bit (not too much) before passing on to something else. Once you've had a good look round – then's the time to come back and buy a whole bar.

When it comes to music of course the world just seems so stuffed with different styles, artists , albums and tracks, and more appearing the whole time, that it gets totally confusing for old gits like (some of) us. What we need is a guide! Enter Mr. Moon. The ideal situation might be to have him tag along whenever you go shopping (or visit the iTunes store) but to be honest this book is pretty close to that. It's like having his musical brain available whenever you're stuck for inspiration. So as well as enjoying more of the same, I've been tuning into some gems I missed along the way and some stuff I could never reasonably have found in more years than this book has pages. The Staple Singers doing "Let me take you there" has been awesome, the Comedy Harmonists version of "Creole Love Call" hilarious and Gwana from Morocco pretty weird but really infectious once you get into it.

Anyway, in mid flow of all this musical meandering, it struck me that this is yet one more way the world is changing – and I'm not talking now about a seemingly endless outpouring of music. It's lists. I never remember my parents having lists of anything – apart from the one that began 2 bags of sugar and ended up with a tin of sardines. I, on the other hand, have had lists for everything for about 25 years. Names, addresses and phone numbers. Family birthdays. Things I have to do pretty soon or face the consequences. Duty rotas. The list (as they say) goes on and on. Now I have to keep a secure list of all my user names and passwords ('cause they're all supposed to be different!). It's not surprising that any password protected web site you visit now has a helpful little button entitled Forgotten your password? Of course I have – what do you expect? Now all these are practical lists, but in such a complicated life, it's not surprising that "those that dish us up our bill of fare" have spotted the need even to have lists to help us relax and be entertained. I'm sure you've noticed the TV obsession with list shows. It's the best of this, the worse of that and the most appalling of the other.

Not to say that this is all a bad thing. My 1000 Recordings book is the follow up to "1000 Places to See Before You Die" which I've also got (sad I know but there you are) and is soon to be followed up, according to the web site, by "1000 Things to Do Before You Die". All useful stuff, but I have to wonder "What would our parents have thought?" Not only was there no cash to partake of any of these various thousands but there probably wasn't the thought that any of it even existed. So isn't it better that we have the choice and can explore and enjoy? Probably, though, as in most of these situations, there's something to gain and something to lose. We may be gaining choice but I can't help feeling we're losing some simplicity.

Coming to New Zealand, we were each allowed 30 kg hold luggage in two items and 5 more hand luggage. With my saxophone taking up one hold item and 12 kg that didn't leave much. But in a funny way it's made things easier. There is now an extremely limited choice of things to wear, books to read, important documents to lose and technology to go wrong. In a way it's all a bit liberating. This is what there is and that's it – make the best of it. A situation, our parents would recognise very well.

So what about the cottage industry of 1000s of this and that? Yeah, I still love the book, I'm still enjoying the music and maybe I'm even interested in what they bring out next. At the same time I have a suggestion. How about "1000 Things You Don't Need and Don't Need to Know" There's bound to be a market out there somewhere.

Plastered and proud of it

It's finally happened. After years of resistance I've finally given in. In fact it's rather been forced upon me but to be honest that's ok. To tell you the truth, I'm even enjoying the experience and feel like an enthusiastic convert wondering why I didn't give in earlier.

Now just to set minds at rest, this isn't Buddhism, Esperanto, the Atkins Diet or Naturism we're talking about - at my age none of these seems like a good idea. It's computers – again. After years of faithful service at the House of Gates, starting with Windows 3.1 up to later incarnations of XP, regularly paying my Office upgrade fees and weeping over system crashes and virus protection as if they were painful but inevitable like creaking joints and mail shots from Saga, I've finally seen the light. I am now a Mac user. That little paper clippy thing that used to drive me up the wall ("you seen to be writing a suicide note – would you like some help with that?") is thankfully now a thing of the past. No longer do I fear the blue screen of death as the entire machine loses consciousness half way through a work of genius I can never re-create. Programmes are stable. I can log on to a wireless network without caring what a domain name is or why it needs to be reset. I can use iTunes with the best of them and get podcasts of Stephen Fry to my heart's content (let's face it - there are many to get). I can use lots of great FREE built in Apple software and download other Open Source stuff without worrying that some teenage hacker in Berlin is at that very moment taking a note of my credit card number to fund his Red Bull habit. The relief is palpable.

As hinted above though, this has all come about a bit by chance – like many of the best discoveries. Being away from home (and desktop computer) for a year, I had to bring the Macbook originally bought more for our boys than me (or alternatively for essential business purposes if Customs and Excise happen to be listening). And with one of them off to Uni and the other swanning around on his gap year (by the way Donald, any idea what mobile phones are for?), the coast was clear. So into the hand luggage it went and after a week or so getting used to it (a bit like driving on the wrong side of the road) Macbook and I are now the best of pals.

However, be that as it may, the thought that came to mind is not to do with Operating System Wars or the evil empire that is Microsoft et al. It's this. What is the word for this phenomenon? So many people swap from PC to Mac (and maybe one or two go back for unaccountable reasons), there ought to be a single word to describe the process - instead of the above 492. So, I could just say I've been macified or macverted or even applied (but not macerated) and everyone would know what I was on about. After all, isn't that what language is supposed to do - give us some means to talk about things that's easier than drawing on the walls and that everyone understands.

Now this isn't a blanket complaint. English generally does pretty well in bushwhacking words from elsewhere or making up new ones. In fact, 2009 has apparently already given us "Carpocalypse" the appalling state of the automotive industry, "momager" a celebrity mum who also serves as business manager and "Jai Ho!" the Hindi equivalent of howzat! In fact, some of us might often feel about half the words and phrases used by our kids have absolutely no meaning, a new meaning or have just been made up on the spot. But it's not true. Throughout its life, English has been adapting to changing needs as all 300 volumes of the Oxford English Dictionary testify.

But sometimes it does let us down. What about the problem folk around our age have in trying to introduce a new significant other of the opposite sex to whom they are not yet married. There is simply no suitable word. Girl or boyfriend makes it sound like you're 17 again. Simply friend isn't enough and partner might be too much. Companion sounds straight out of Jane Austen and mate smacks too much of David Attenborough. So we're left fumbling with "Eh, hi Sandy. Have you met, Samantha? We're … eh … we're … eh … going out … sort of – ish." Not quite satisfactory is it?

And there's more. What about the couple of hours which are later than afternoon and earlier than evening - teatime only works if you're actually having some tea. Or some proper words for wine instead of those recycled from fruit, flowers and cigar boxes. Or the first decade of the 21st century - the noughties sounds ridiculous and constantly calling it "the first decade of the 21st century" takes up so much time that soon we'll be needing a word for the second decade of the 21st century. And there are other concepts for which we have far too many words. Like being drunk for example which makes use of blotto / blootered / pie-eyed / steaming / guttered / legless / paralytic / sozzled / wasted and so on. In fact my brief Internet research tells me there are at least 141 variants with more being thought up all the time.

So here's my suggestion. Excessive alcohol consumption has had overly generous treatment from the English language so clearly won't miss a few of its synonyms. My Mac-ness could use a spare. Henceforth when trying to explain my conversion to anyone interested (and many who aren't), I plan to tell them I've been "plastered" and hope it catches on. In the meantime it may serve the double purpose of saving me from scandal. So - ill informed friend: "I met Les down the town last night – he was absolutely plastered." Better informed friend: "Yes – I know. He was telling me. Apparently when you're plastered you don't need virus protection any more." Wonderful.

Kiwis Roasting by an Open Fire

In the midst of trying to choose between alternative topics for this month's ramble I've been hit with an awful realisation. Let me explain.

My first choice was "My Day as Frodo Baggins" – or – "How my travelling companions had to help me up the slopes of Mount Doom (otherwise known as Mount Ngauruhoe in the Tongariro National Park, New Zealand)" The good news is that my wedding ring did not glow red hot, suddenly weigh a ton or burn the image of evil former work colleagues into my mind. The bad news is that, much like Frodo, I needed almost bodily dragged up by people not much younger than me but a whole lot fitter.

My other option was "Bitten! My Adventures with the New Zealand White Tail Spider" – a bit like the black widow but a different colour and still happily married. Apparently this is the one real nasty poisonous thing the length and breath of the "Land of the Long White Cloud" yet it chose to spent a night on the town crawling over my sleeping form before sinking its equally nasty poisonous fangs into the back of my right hand. The next morning it was a bit itchy. The morning after that it was the size of a basketball and a trip to the Doc was required. Now, a courses of anti-histamines, antibiotics and anti-inflammatories later (not yet anti-depressants but that may come) normal service has been resumed.

Anyway – in the middle of spinning a plate to see which to home in on, it suddenly struck me. Blimey – it's only weeks till Christmas – so all other material goes on the back burner. Now the fact that early December is only weeks from Christmas is not of itself that much of a revelation. To be fair we do get reasonable warning. Roughly the same timescale applied last December and the December before that right back to 350 AD when Pope Julius I decided on Dec. 25th. Contrary to what you might think, Julius did not wake up one day in late November and wonder how he could get the latest Wii game without having to pay for it (unlike most Christmas recipients nowadays). Rather, December 25th was settled on to allow pagans of the day who were used to having a knees-up around that time of year to keep on with the merrymaking while putting a Christian face on it – should they so desire. So not much change there then.

Anyway, the point about Christmas fiendishly creeping up on us isn't to do with its actual unpredictability. (By the way, what a terrifying thought that is – if you actually didn't know when it was going to be until the day before when it was announced on the radio like the new Number One.) It's just that life is busy and before you know it, here we are again. And there are a few other pointers to keep you right. Like driving to work in the dark then back home again still in the dark like pit ponies. Or stormy weather and the boats all cancelled again. Or cranking up the heating as if oil really were going out of fashion – as indeed we'd all like it to.

Now that is well and good and no doubt alerts most reasonably conscious citizens to the fact that something vaguely Christmassy will be going on soon. Or it would do if you happen to be in the northern hemisphere. And there's the rub. S l o w l y, it is beginning to warm up here, gardens are blooming, beach parties are being planned, folks are organising their summer holidays and everybody's getting a bit more cheerful. All things that by rights should be happening in June – not December! It's ridiculous. I simply can't get used to the thought that Christmas holidays and summer holidays are one and the same. In fact, breaking up early (as students do) we had Christmas dinner on November 21st. How daft is that? My kids moan loudly if I tell them I'm beginning to feel a bit Christmassy around Dec. 13th! How could they cope?

But in spite of all the differences, the really funny thing is that no matter how out of kilter the seasons are, there is still a big effort to make things like Christmas should be. Christmas cards are still all holly, snowmen, Santa, reindeer and whatnot, not beach BBQs and flowers in full bloom as would make more sense. There is currently a huge Christmas tree downtown and Christmas lights slung across the road. And, yes, people are ordering turkeys to be eaten in weather better suited to salad and ice cream.

And that's the interesting thing about it. Despite everything to the contrary, we love the familiar. Especially when we're far from home, we want things to be as much like home as they can be, even if it means ignoring the natural cycle and pretending it's freezing cold when it's actually 32 in the shade. Maybe that's why Invercargill – the most southern city in New Zealand (and hence the coldest and most inclement) - was a popular settling point for northerners. It was the nearest thing to home they could find with a similar climate which meant similar farming practices and similar lifestyle.

So, despite it all, just like these 19th century migrants, I'm going to stick to the familiar. It's going to be turkey and all the trimmings, brightly wrapped pressies all round, In the Bleak Midwinter on the CD player and an after dinner snooze. On the beach.

Dear Santa ... thanks

36, Sheen St.
Roslyn
Dunedin
New Zealand

Dear Santa

You must be so relieved it's all over for another year! The sleigh is in for its MOT, Rudolph and Co. are lounging around bragging about how they fooled air traffic control yet again, the Elves have all cleared off to Hawaii till July and your letter box is no longer stuffed with several tons of begging letters. In short, you are probably saying to yourself, "Thank goodness that's over. Absolutely, positively never again." In that frame of mind, you may not want to be bothered with any more Christmas correspondence, however I thought it only decent to write and say thank you as I imagine not many do.

First of all, a preliminary thanks for noting our change of address. I entirely understand you weren't able to reply to my email however everything got here safely enough so it obviously got through. Then, moving on to the main event, an even bigger thank you for all the lovely presents. The Homer Simpson socks are nice and very welcome. The Bart Simpson tie likewise. The Marg Simpson apron and Lisa cookbook I may make less use of but I'm sure it's the thought that counts – even for Santa. Books are always welcome so thank you for The Humourous History of Company Law, 365 Hilarious Auditing Anecdotes, The Wit and Wisdom of Jordan (quite short but well illustrated) and John Humphrey's Fashion Hints for the Over Fifties. These are currently stacked by my bedside awaiting perusal apart from those few propping up the wobbly leg on the kitchen table.

You'll be pleased to know that I've already been enjoying the Grumpy Old Men DVDs though I'm a bit mystified as to why three copies. Never mind – very funny anyway and I so agree with Rick Wakeman's complaints about pointless and useless gadgets. Thanks also for the nose hair clippers and Avocado peeler. I hope you don't mind that I've given the Skateboard to the boy next door and Every Boy's Book of Classic Cars to Cameron Stout. The tangerine I have eaten and the Reindeer Droppings I assume were meant to be some sort of joke.

Now, if you don't mind Santa, a word of two about the items I thought I had included in my Letter to You but somehow didn't arrive. Surely it was all clear enough in the bullet lists on pages 4 and 5. Anyway, the end result is that I may need to spend some of my own Christmas money from kind relations, a less than ideal situation as I'm sure you'll agree. Just to refresh your memory we're talking about the Complete Star Trek DVDs (all three generations with bonus movies), two tickets for Status Quo's next final farewell tour (special Australian mystery guest) and the bright red Fender Strat copy with carry case, spare strings and 32 page Ageing Rock Star Easy Chords Playalong instruction book. And a pony. Now I find it hard to imagine these items were not in stock as your marvellous elves seem able to produce all sorts of junk the kids next door neither need nor deserve and certainly will not appreciate. Nor do I think it likely that I could have fallen foul of the "Have you been a good middle aged man?" clause (or Claus?) as certain items did arrive exactly as ordered. I have always understood the good behaviour stipulation to be a sort of all or nothing thing i.e. good conduct = presents : bad conduct = lumps of coal with nothing in between. A bit like how you can't be only slightly pregnant. But perhaps I'm mistaken.

So my suggestion, Santa, which I hope you'll agree is a win-win sort of thing, is that you consider instituting some sort of reprise event in about six months time. This would be highly welcomed here in the southern hemisphere where people have to put up with endless barbecuing on the beach in December but no presents whatever to brighten the dark days of July. I would not insist on submitting another entire list but be quite content with those items missing from your first delivery. This would incidentally present a further marketing opportunity which, in this day and age, not even magical beings can afford to ignore. With the recession biting, there are bound to be plenty of applicants for "Santa's Grotto" staff, which, since I assume is some sort of franchised business, might also bring in a bit of much needed off season income.

And while we're at it, I wonder if you might be open to a few remarks on branding of some of your other lines. Several female member of the extended family got perfume this year (again) with brand names I frankly find rather disturbing. They all seem to be called things like Addiction, Obsession or Poison etc. Forgive me if I'm wrong but I thought these were supposed to be bad things. Imagine "Poison" on a packet of fish cakes and you'll see my point. I'm sure today's modern woman would be much happier with something more pleasant like Alpine or Cornfields. In fact the same formulation could probably be used for perfume and toilet cleaner which would represent considerable efficiency savings.

Anyway Santa, can I thank you once again for all your hard work in the year just gone and your more than 90% success rate. Regards to Rudolph and all the others whose names escape me. Best wishes to the Elves when they come back and if you need any advice on future projects you know where I can be found.

Best wishes

Les

P.S. Would you be interested in a joint venture to take over responsibility for Father's Day?

Decapitate Peter, Electrocute Paul...

We are currently suffering from a plague of flies. When you're shivering under a blanket of snow - however deep and crisp and even - you long for a couple of flies as an indicator of warming - if not global at least in the living room. But though a couple of flies might not be so bad, plagues of them are almost always unwelcome. So, a middle aged man's mind turns to thoughts of flyecide. But how?

I'd like to say no flies were hurt in the writing of this column but I'm hoping it won't be true. Whatever works is good. Electrocuted, squashed, poisoned, paralysed, blown up, ripped apart, starved to death, drowned or decapitated. It probably doesn't make much difference to flykind and it certainly makes no difference to me. Flies will die - with a bit of luck. Only effectiveness and speed of delivery are at issue. It's the Cowan lunch at stake here, not insect welfare.

So, method one - no doubt something you've tried yourself at home. Creep up behind them palm open. Gently move in for the kill. Wait till you can see the blacks of their eyes. Then STRIKE! Dag nab it - fly boy escapes to land one more time on the cold chicken salad. Ok, tactic two. Same as tactic one but with a newspaper. Maybe it was the proximity of warm human flesh that gave the game away. I'm using an International copy of the Daily Mail to avoid any possibility of warmth. Yes! Yes! No! No! No! Some success but still an inadequate hit rate. Back to the drawing board.

Now what was it my late father-in-law used with such devastating effectiveness? Ah yes. Rubber bands. A quick trip to the stationary supplies drawer and I am all tooled up. Lock and Load. All Right. Here we go. Mistaking myself for one of the Rubber Band of Brothers I get the mother and father of all elastic weaponry out and load up. Actually it's harder than you think. You have to draw said band back against a finger nail then bend the finger to the right angle, otherwise the band shoots off at too high an angle and only has the slimmest chance of knocking off a fly on the ceiling not the intended victim at all. This would be ok as a dead fly is a dead fly wherever but since the odds are so poor, it's probably still not on. Anyway - back at rubber band HQ, we mount our weapon, cock the aiming mechanism - in this case my left thumb - and let fly (as it were). Dang. Fly - 1 Rubber Band Artillery - Nil. Then I remember wife's father had a specially constructed launching mechanism (a stick) and a bag of specially specified ammunition that came with it. That might be it. Or he might have just had more practice. Or was naturally better at it. I try a few more times but without success. So what now? Brute force proves inadequate so – it's time for brains. No contest (we hope). Quiet at the back. Let's analyse the problem. Flies are landing on my lunch. This is not an acceptable situation. Could we not use this fly behaviour against them like Steven Seagal whirling baddies through plate glass windows by subtly diverting their furious charges with an Aikido sidestep. Perhaps I could make my chicken salad poisonous to flies? That might work but could also run the risk of collateral damage to Coalition Forces - the so badly misnamed "friendly fire".

Well what about if we could entice the flies to nibble on something tasty but deadly that we are not about to eat? Like girls who get rid of unwanted suitors by palming them off on a friend who goes for anything in trousers but leaves them wishing they'd stayed in the watch Top of the Pops or wash their hair. Anyone who has ever eaten outdoors knows, flies love jam. Spread some best strawberry on your pancake and it instantly sends out enticing messages stronger than the sight of an overweight celebrity to a Heat magazine photographer. Flies land on jam, get stuck, remain struggling vainly but unnoticed by picnickers until eaten. Right on! We've got a jar of apricot jelly bought in a moment of weakness when I was fruitlessly looking for marmalade. Not perfect but worth trying. I liberally smear a side plate and position it directly across the final approach flight path. And wait. Flies are landing on my arm, my hand, my elbow, my knee. Even my face. But not on the apricot stuff. Perhaps if I spread apricot goo all over my arm, hand, elbow, knee and face...

Anyway, while I'm obsessing about flies and about to go for the hoover, I have a quick look at the BBC website. News about Haiti is coming in. A magnitude 7 quake has just hit followed by aftershocks. The Red Cross says up to 3 million people may be affected. An estimated 1.5 million people have been left homeless.

Suddenly fly problems don't seem so important.

Greeks, Geeks and Light Bulb Moments

"Eureka!" shouted Archimedes, jumping out the bath and running down the street stark naked. Or so the legend goes. Having been troubled for some time with the knotty problem of calculating the volume of irregular objects, the great Greek got out of the tub one day and noticed, as he did so, that the water level had dropped by an amount exactly equal to the volume of himself that had been under it. Had he been a Scot he would probably have shouted "Jings, crivens and help ma bob" but instead, having the good luck to be born in the land of ouzo and kebabs, he let fly with "I've found it!" - or "Eureka!" as they put it then.

And ever since, eureka has been the expletive of choice when something new and exciting appears - or something old and missing reappears. So, when you've been hunting all day for your glasses / wallet / wedding ring / passport / car keys or winning lottery ticket, then it turns up in your inside jacket pocket - exactly where you left it - eureka! Or, in the story of the minister who was convinced someone had stolen his bike and thought the way to deal with this was to preach through the ten commandments until he got to "Thou shalt not steal" when he hoped the guilty party would be stricken with remorse and own up. As it happened he got to "Thou shalt not commit adultery" and remembered where he'd left it. Eureka.

Anyway, I've recently had a eureka moment myself. You'd have thought that after a career in social services then running a business, I'd have had my personality tested within an inch of its life over the years. But no. Apart from those who consider your correspondent merely a "grumpy old git" or "as much use as a rusty hacksaw on an airbed", I've always managed to avoid personality tests. You know the sort of thing. You look at a child's accident with a paint pot and tell the bloke in the lab coat why it reminds you of Marilyn Monroe. Or you fill in the blanks in a 50 page questionnaire to discover why you hate being late, prefer to keep your pencils nicely sharpened and can't do algebra. To be specific, I've been doing a course recently that involved working through the personality test at: www.humanmetrics.com/cgi-win/JTypes2.asp

After remarkably few questions, the site purports to come up with your personality type in terms of how "Introvert / Extrovert" or "Thinker / Feeler" you might be (and a few other things I won't bore you with), finally ending up with 4 letters and some percentages that are supposed to sum you up to a tee.

Now, in normal circumstances, I would tend to be pretty skeptical of that sort of thing - surely the world is a more complicated place and the 6,692,030,277 (and counting) of us far too rich and various to be limited to 16 types based on a score for each of 8 values. But, like I said, it turned out to be a truly eureka moment. For me at least - and a good few others - it actually seemed to work. So we all sat around for a bit with our collective gobs hanging open thinking "Wow - that's why I love this, hate that, find something else boring or exciting and can't stand my brother / sister / boss or mother-in-law (by the way, it was somebody else thinking that last one - **not me**!).

Anyway, what my personality type might actually be is probably only of interest to me and those who have to put up with it. The point is that from time to time eureka moments come along. Among all the routine of work, family and trying to survive economic crises (which, much like buses, seem to come along all at once), there are occasional moments when the light bulb goes on and things suddenly appear in a different light. Which is fun. My own eureka moment has actually had quite a surprising effect. It's helped me see some things in a much more positive light and made sense of some others that up to now had been quite confusing and uncomfortable. So eureka moments are great, which, based on a sample of one, has led me a to few conclusions:

- there is definitely more than one way of making sense of things
- you're never too old to change your point of view
- being open minded and curious seems to help
- sometimes changing your point of view is better, quicker and easier than changing the world around about you

Then there's also the eureka moment that happens to someone else, which you'd think we would approve of and encourage. One of my pet hates - and we're talking pet elephants more than hamsters here - is the phrase that someone has suddenly "got religion". What gives any of us the right to sum up someone else's eureka moment as if it were a dose of the flu? Not all eurekas are spiritual of course, far from it, but some are, and it seems to me that they too should be treated with respect.

Anyway, you might be thinking "ok fair enough but what's the point?" Well here are a few things that are all supposed to have come about in eureka moments, any one of which I would be quite happy to be remembered for - Post-It Notes, Velcro, Alternating Current, Relativity, the Theory of Gravity and Paul McCartney's tune for "Yesterday".

So, if you fancy inventing a revolutionary material, writing a million seller or just being a bit more comfortable with yourself, turn the lights down low, put some soft music on, run a bath and let your mind freewheel. Just keep a bath robe handy in case you need to tell the world.

Of Passwords, PINs and Internet Protection.

Do you remember when the Berlin Wall came down, when the bad old Soviet Union ceased to be and the Cold War was won? All that talk about perestroika, the world being a safer place and the peace dividend (which mainly seemed to involve shipyard workers losing their jobs)? Well, I've been reflecting recently on whether my world is a safer place and come to the conclusion that there seem to be man more nasties out there than I can remember back in 1989. Granted I'm not living in a war zone or subject to terrorism in my own backyard, but there is one particularly nasty bit of the world I don't need to go looking for as it has a persistent habit of coming to me. And that's the sort of nastiness that comes at you over cyberspace.

The reason for these gloomy thoughts is that the desktop file I keep for all my Internet passwords, User Names, login IDs, security questions (and answers), Sitekey identities, PIN numbers, email addresses, registration numbers, security codes and other such stuff is currently standing at seven pages. That's right. Seven. I don't think my parents possessed a single password or ID their entire life barring a national insurance number and a ration book. Their parents wouldn't have known what a password was. But now the world's a safer place, there are people from all over the globe trying to steal my name, identity, email address and entire web presence not to mention emptying my bank account and changing the locks on anyplace I might frequent online. It feels like the cyber equivalent of camping by the roadside somewhere you wouldn't want to drive through after dark without an armed escort.

So I have seven pages of passwords. In fact I tend to use the same passwords - or minor variations - much more than you're supposed to so it should actually be much longer. Let's face it, the chances of actually remembering more than one in five of all the passwords I need is negligible, hence the need for a file, which is of course also password protected. Just to spell it out, the reason this is all necessary is because there are so many crooks out there just waiting for some of my personal data left lying about unprotected. It reminds me of the bears in A.A. Milne's famous "Lines and Squares": "And the little bears growl to each other, 'He's mine / As soon as he's silly and steps on a line.' "

When were you last robbed in the street or had your car broken into? I hope it was a long time ago. But however unlucky or careless you've been you wouldn't expect it to be happening on a daily basis. But this is exactly the situation online. Every single day I get emails, which if I answered or opened, would put me at risk of being robbed or defrauded. Several times a week gentlemen from Nigeria tell me I've been left a cool million and just need to send them my bank details to have the funds transferred. Every few days I get an email purporting to be from a major bank asking me to review and update my bank details or credit card PIN. Our son recently expressed an interest in a very nice reasonably priced rented flat in Edinburgh. He sensibly asked our advice and since it seemed too good to be true, we wondered whether it actually was too good to be true. Turns out the property didn't exist, the alleged landlord was unregistered and the council had had a stream of similar problems. In other words - scam. Last year I had a very positive email from a US publisher offering to handle my beloved novel manuscript subject to a little professional editing. A bit of further digging turned up dozens of complaints. Scam.

But what am I complaining about? A fool and his money have always been easily parted, no harm was actually done and I believe my grandmother was swindled out of her life savings in New York around 1910. What's different? Several things. Firstly this level of harassment is of a totally different order to anything any of us has every experienced before. If this were happening in the real world I would think law and order had totally broken down and I was living in the middle of a drug war in a banana republic. Secondly, this might be something you and I can handle (being informed and wily cyber surfers) but maybe our mums and dads, aunts, uncles and grandparents aren't quite so on the ball and could easily suffer real damage and loss. Thirdly, it makes us all a lot more tolerant of casual crime, which I do not think we should accept as normality. Why, as a society, are we prepared to tolerate an entire slab of our lives being subject to virtually constant assault and accept it as part of normal daily life?

Rumour has it that an election may be in the offing. What could a new administration do to improve my lot in life - besides the usual lower taxes, higher employment and better services? Here's a suggestion. Identify the brightest and the most persistent spammers and Internet fraudsters and put them on the payroll. Then give them whatever facilities they need to make the lives of anyone still involved in this nasty business an utter misery. General elections usually involve a lot of hot air about safer streets and toughness on crime. Personally I would be overjoyed just to be able to open my mailbox and find nothing but offers for medication I may not need and tickets I can't afford, without tempting offers from the World Investment Bank in Lagos. Anyone want to pick up the challenge? Alistair - are you out there?

A fishy tale - with plenty of salt and vinegar please!

It's funny what you miss when you can't get it any more. Having been out of the UK for the best part of a year now, I'm beginning to get serious withdrawal symptoms. As Joni Mitchell succinctly put it "Don't it always seem to go that you don't know what you've got till it's gone..." Not to miss the UK weather is of course proverbial, though nowadays it seems we have to include fire, flood, earthquakes and volcanoes in the list of natural phenomena we'd rather do without! I'm also not missing the election you won't be surprised to know. For the first time in my adult life I'm not going to be voting, and not just because I haven't bothered to get a postal vote sorted. Like many of us, I've just succumbed to a general fed-up-ness with the whole shebang. A plague on all your duck houses is all I can say right now.

So what am I actually missing? Well there's family, friends, and so on (all the worthy things I ought to miss and really, really do - honest). But for some unaccountable reason, what I'm actually craving is something altogether humbler. It's a good fish supper. It's embarrassing not to have a worthier object in mind, but that's the fact. It's a good crisp, mouthwateringly succulent, melt in your mouth, salt and vinegary, generously proportioned, newspaper wrapped haddock nestling on a golden bed of tasty chips. Now don't tell me you don't fancy a fish supper right now after that!

There is of course something called fish and chips in New Zealand but it simply ain't the same. For example, I've discovered that the humble haddock - in my opinion the uncrowned king of battered beauty - just doesn't hang around in the Southern Ocean. In fact, melanogrammus aeglefinus, better known as the Atlantic haddock (which kind of gives the game away), apparently thrives from Cape Hatteras in North Carolina to Greenland with the highest concentration along the U.S. coast on George's Bank. Not anywhere around the "Land of the Long White Cloud". Which makes it the land of the long sad face for fish and chip lovers.

My web site source of haddock intelligence (that's intelligence about haddock, not haddock who are actually intelligent - which may exist but so far have been bright enough to keep themselves off the menu) tells

146

me that this species "spawns on offshore banks and is characterized by an extremely high fecundity and extensive variability in annual recruitment." Well, I can tell you they are far from fecund anywhere about here and recent recruitment drives, far from being variable, have uniformly failed to attract a single applicant. Ok, they have other things they dump on top of your chips in the hope that nobody used to the real thing will notice. There's hoki, snapper, tarakihi, akaroa and a few others even less pronounceable but even if they were equal to the haddock (no fears of that) what you get is a piece the size of a fish finger - not even an entire fish hand - on top of about a ton of lack lustre chips - and no salt or vinegar. Of course there have been times hope triumphs over realism - always, only to be disappointed. And I'm not alone in this. I've actually found a web discussion forum solely devoted (sorry 'bout that one) to the lack of decent fish 'n' chips in the entire Southern Hemisphere.

Of course, once you start to think about it, this whole business of missing things back home opens up a huge can of worms. Imagine the feelings of those displaced from home and all things familiar and dumped in the colonies a few hundred years ago as a result of the destruction of the clan system, clearances, orphan resettlement, transportation or just all round poverty and my longing for a good tray of fish and chips pales somewhat into insignificance. I recently uncovered a journal written by my great grandfather describing 19th century travels to the USA and back and I can only marvel at the determination, fortitude and self-reliance of people travelling such enormous distances in more primitive times often with no real hope of ever getting back home. If you didn't take it with you and they didn't have it there then you did without. Or alternatively you might try to invent, discover or recreate what you were missing. Hence the thriving Scottish cultures still surviving in Nova Scotia, Canada, the US, Australia and here in New Zealand. In fact, I've been told that per head of population there are more pipers in New Zealand than in Scotland and I wouldn't be surprised. There might well be a stronger motivation to tackle the Pibroch in Paeroa than in Perth.

And if things went wrong in the new adopted land there isn't a lot to be done about it. I believe my grandmother went to New York in the early 1900s with a sum of money to invest to provide for her livelihood. Unfortunately, she tried to buy a property to set up as a boarding house from a man who didn't actually own it. So, having lost everything, she ended up working as a children's nurse in an orphanage in rural Pennsylvania until it changed its function to a care home for elderly people and she eventually become a resident. There weren't too many options for a young widow with a small daughter to support.

So, maybe I need to keep my fish and chips in perspective. Life can be unpredictable and the old fashioned capacity to "make the best of it" might make the difference between survival and giving up entirely. Having said that - I'm still planning to find out the nearest chippy to the airport on touchdown in about 2 month's time. My mouth is watering at the thought. The only question is - can I stop at one?

Stretchy, Para and Roller Thingies

Although I have no idea where you might be reading this, it's probably going to be somewhere safe, comfortable, relaxed and a bit laid back. Maybe you've got your feet up while your nearest and dearest (or else family members too young to protest) are about to bring you a cup of tea and tasty slice of buttery toast. Maybe you're at work catching up on local events when we all know you ought to be working. But having finally found a corner of the office / garage / workshop / slatted byre where you can't be spotted from the boss's room / head mechanic's bay / Chief Executive's Dept., frankly who cares? Possibly you are even up to however many chins in warm soapy water easing away the pain of the day while relatives queue up outside with legs crossed shouting encouragement through the keyhole. (Actually, my father was in the habit of disappearing into the loo with the Sunday Post and only emerging once Oor Wullie, The Broons, Merry Mac's Fun Parade and the Hon Man had all been polished off. By which time calls of nature were being met next door.) Anyway, whatever your choice, you're enjoying a bit of peace and quiet and not anticipating anything nasty in the next five minutes.

On the other hand, also as you are reading this, a good friend of mine may be sitting nervously at fifteen thousand feet waiting for someone to push her out of an aeroplane supported only by a nylon sheet the size of a couple of bath mats and a ball of string. Why? Because apparently that's what people do for fun these days. In fact, an otherwise perfectly sensible younger relative recently got a parachute jump as a special birthday present only on condition she got the DVD as well. Is that supposed to convey love and affection or simply a desire to see you lose your cool, your lunch, your false teeth and possibly your underwear all in one go?

But apparently this is now a widespread form of entertainment. For only the cost of an arm and a leg (which seems appropriate somehow) you can jump out of aeroplanes or off very high mountains, with something not much bigger than a lunchbox on your back containing everything you need not to end up at the bottom like hairy strawberry jam. You can go rafting in water white or black. White water means you get soaked, agitated like a milk shake, possibly dunked in fast flowing water, banged off rocks the size of a VW Beetle and frozen half to death. With black water, nobody hears you scream 'cause the whole thing happens underground and you may never get out at all.

We are all familiar with the good old bungee jump which aims to make your innards outards, but now there's apparently an even whiter knuckle variety called the rocket bungee where they shoot you up before the long drop so you can experience multiple Gs in both directions. And also leak in both directions. There's also the static bungee where they strap you into something like a gigantic rubber band attached to a couple of pylons, ramp up the tension then let go. Someone I know (I promised not to tell), found the rubber harness round their reproductive bits didn't quite fit and had to endure 30 or 40 boings before they could put everything back where nature intended as well as checking for long term damage. My personal favourite however in the "entertainment as torture" genre is the hamster ball in which you get strapped into a plastic globe the size of a greenhouse and pushed down a steep incline. I imagine somebody is employed at the bottom to let you out and clean up afterwards.

Now what do all these activities have in common, apart from the fact they cost a small fortune, appeal overwhelmingly to the under 25s and would (collectively) be the last thing I would want to do on earth? Well, clearly, they are about something that feels incredibly dangerous but actually isn't really. So, although your brain may understand this is only a mild to moderate risk, the adrenal gland has yet to get the good news and so churns out adrenaline by the bucket load. Now, correct me if I'm wrong but I've always thought that progress was aimed at trying to eliminate that sort of thing. So about 12,000 years ago, a day when you were not pursued by a sabre-tooth tiger was a good day. The adrenaline rush was meant to give you the extra edge to clear the bushes or jump the gorge to get away for quick, sharp, hairy things that wanted you as the nearest thing to steak tartar. But better not to have to.

But now something funny seems to have happened. Apparently, with all that running, hiding, spearing and clubbing, some of us have kind of got a taste for it. But nowadays, anything actually involving any serious level of challenge, is rendered impossible by paperwork heavier than the apparatus itself. Obviously nobody wants our young people subject to more real risks as a result of which people die, inevitably just by the way of averages, but some people seem to need a risk involving stretchy, para and roller thingies. And, despite my absolute horror of it all, I think I have to say good on them. Good on them for taking a day off safety first and letting absolutely everything hang out. And I think we over 40s could take a lesson from them. Maybe we all need a bit more risk from time to time just to savour the zest of living. I certainly intend to, just as soon as I've finished this cup of tea and slice of toast. Definitely. Or, probably. At least possibly...

Pens, Paper and Facebook Friends

Anyone who hasn't spent the last thirty years in outer space or marooned on Love Island knows we're living in the Information Age. Whatever there is to know about anything - we now know more of it than anyone else in history - with all that information instantly available. My random web searches on Begonia, Beatles and Barbecue produced 1,820,000, 54,300,000 and 36,700,000 hits respectively in about 0.2 seconds each. In the case of any of them I could probably grown old and die before reading a tenth of it. So you would probably think that anything that could possibly count as information is bound to be in more plentiful supply than ever before. Wrong. I've recently stumbled on something truly informative that used to be part of almost everybody's life but has now almost entirely disappeared. It's not the secret knowledge of the druids or even the contents of Latin volumes nobody can read any more. It's the humble, hand written, personal letter.

Now I'm well aware that the Post Office delivers millions more "items" than ever before - but how many of them are real letters? Almost none. What we get is a deluge of pseudo post from banks, insurers, marketing companies and a million catalogue distributors. But nobody we actually know writing personally to us. And that's a very big change. Letter writing used to be very common. Children to parents and back again, sweethearts to each other, friends to friends, business contacts and even total strangers to people they had something to say to. That's not to say of course that the sum of interpersonal communication has decreased - quite the opposite with the ghastly phenomenon of social networking. Facebook and its ilk seem to mostly thrive on gossip, backbiting, backstabbing, snide remarks and downright abuse. Better to call it "anti-social networking". It's the electronic equivalent of road rage where just because you're behind the keyboard of a computer it seems to be ok to say things you would never say directly to a living person for fear of a punch on the nose. But the destructive effect can be the same.

But I digress. Personal correspondence is down. Total communication via email, networking, phone and text is hugely up. So what's the problem? Well, this train of thought comes about by having just read a wonderful collection of letters by a very interesting person. Joy

152

Davidman may not be well known by that name, however, if I tell you in later life she became Mrs. C.S. Lewis and was partly the subject of the very successful film "Shadowlands" then bells might ring. Lewis and Davidman met in late middle age and had a short but intense romance before her early death. Her collected letters "Out of my Bone" written over about thirty years are a fascinating record not only of her life, and growing relationship with Lewis but also of the times she lived in. Along the way we hear of her typing the manuscript of Lewis's famous Screwtape Letters or that a new book in the children's Narnia stories has just been completed or that they are having lunch with T.S. Eliot or a pint of the best with Arthur C. Clarke (who has just become divorced from his nightclub hostess wife of 18 months to whom he will be paying $5,000 per year allowance!) Besides this there is all of Davidman's own wit and wisdom alongside efforts to cope with lone parenthood, struggles to make ends meet and eventually her losing battle with cancer.

Now of course writing by hand still more or less survives so a collection by some interesting 21st century figure is still entirely possible, but the fact is that it's just hugely less likely than a generation ago. It is just so much easier and convenient to bang off a quick email. It's quicker, more convenient to reply to and easier to keep track of. What's not to like? Well - an envelope with your name on it that someone has addressed by hand, filled with a three page letter they've just sat down at the kitchen table and written, stuck a stamp on and dropped in a post box - that's what. It's the very inconvenience and effort I appreciate. Someone was thinking of me and took the time and effort not to send an email. Wonderful.

And I recently received and appreciated just such a letter - probably the first in years. An old (i.e. former - not actually old) university pal we had spend New Year with heard that my Mum had just passed away and wrote by way of condolence. But rather than just a card and a brief "thinking of you at this sad time" (though that would also have been appreciated), they took the time and effort to sympathise, chat, update, comment, question, joke, laugh (on paper) and express something of our own thirty years of friendship. Whatever else it does well, email just isn't the same.

So, what you get a glimpse of in a letter is relationship expressed with pen, paper, stamps and envelopes, journeys to the post box, delivery by the post man and the pleasure of receiving, opening, reading and keeping that letter over most of a lifetime. Compared to that the invitation to be someone's "friend" on Facebook somehow doesn't quite cut the mustard.

Fashion Victims of the World Unite!

You'd have thought "That doesn't go" was one of my mother's favourite phrases. It was certainly one I heard a lot. Aged 12 or so, there I was in my mauve fair Isle jumper, salmon pink trousers, suede boots and parka all set for the 35th Stirlingshire Scout's Christmas record hop (what used to entertain the yooff before the days of disco). But Mum said it didn't go. Which meant neither did I.

Since the exact meaning of "going" was never fully explained, just what didn't go and why was always something of a mystery. Hence the following typical exchange…

> **Me**: That's me off Mum. See you.
> **Mum**: Just a minute. That doesn't go.
> **Me**: What do you mean? What doesn't go?
> **Mum**: That. It doesn't go. Look in the mirror.
> **Me**: I did. It's fine.
> **Mum**: No it's not. It doesn't go.
> **Me**: Yes it does
> **Mum**: It does not. Go and change!

And so on. No prizes for guessing who had the casting vote in all such debates.

Not that anyone could accuse Mum of being a fashionista. She was a decent respectable Scottish Mum who did her best to make ends meet which meant very little room for fancy footwear, showy shirts, jazzy jackets or trendy togs in general . We got sensible shoes, serviceable trousers and white bri-nylon shirts, the best the Co-op boys' section or Dillon's men's outfitters had to offer. The very thought makes me feel like scratching. In any event, certainly not a new pair of shiny black wet look boots like Craig Esplin took delight in showing off outside double tech drawing the first day back after the summer hols. Grrr!

But even allowing for the limited range that did make it through the survival of what fitteth, there were still things that simply didn't go. Apparently. It was something to do with colour I think. Some shades were thought to "clash" with others. They offended the eye of the beholder. They didn't offend my eye but that didn't matter. It's like the definition I came across recently - a cardigan is something you put on when your mum feels cold. Even though Mum would not actually be accompanying me to the dance, she still retained right of veto on what the outside world could be expected to put up with.

Of course, this position on "going" wasn't always consistent but bearing in mind the rules of growing up, kids are not allowed to challenge parents by applying the same standard the other way round. In true 70s style we had a patterned carpet, different patterned wallpaper and no two pieces of furniture from the same era. But all of that still apparently "went" while my fair isle jumper and heat seeking trousers didn't. Mum just had her own style rules and that was that - probably dictated by what was worn out and what else was on sale at the time. Which is fair enough. But, on the other hand, that's also not to say that we were totally devoid of style sense, in fact mum even had a colour I have never heard anyone else refer to then or since. Helio. I have since discovered it's a reference to the heliotrope, a bush with vivid purple coloured flowers. Lots of things in Mum's world were helio though nobody else ever referred to it. I used to wonder whether it was a pigment of her imagination.

All of which is a somewhat laboured excuse for why I still remain mystified by the murky world of style and colour. If only Mum had explained why things didn't go, life could have been so much different. If she had spelled it all out and I had somehow grasped it, what might not have followed? I could have been stylish for goodness sake! Even despite growing up in the decade fashion forgot. Think of it. Central Scotland's Bryan Ferry or David Bowie. Hopefully not Gary Glitter of course.

But then, having to have it explained to you probably means you just don't have it. A bit like if you have to ask how much it is, then you probably can't afford it. Maybe I have to face the fact that there's more to it than the fact that fair isle jumpers and salmon pink trousers are not acceptable teenage gear in any era. So, it wasn't really Mum's fault at all. I was just at the back of the queue when they were dishing out essence of cool. My dress code DNA was lacking and my genes weren't selfish enough to make sure I always wore Levis. Verified by the fact that as I'm typing this I'm listening to the soundtrack from Saturday Night Fever, Shocking isn't it?

To clean or not to clean

- that is the question

What seems like a long, long time ago now, we used to celebrate this time of year with kids going back to school, no more summer holiday childcare (hurray) and normal family service resumed. Working from home, that used to mean shoving our boys through the air lock 30 seconds before bus time then putting the kettle on for a second cuppa and checking email in my pyjamas. Now, we seem to have finally passed into the next phase of life with younger son delivered to halls of residence and ourselves officially registered as "footloose and fancy free".

In the process, however, we also had a few nights camping with older son who has been in his flat for a few years already and spent July and August working like a trojan to try and keep body and soul together for yet another year of juggling practice. Sorry - academic achievement.

Anyway, close your eyes and imagine a student flat with six occupants several years into the tenancy. What do you see? A fridge well stocked with penicillin perhaps. Worktops with enough debris of former meals to make a six course dinner for two (or a two course dinner for six?), and still have plenty left for the dog. Toilets that would make Monty Python's depiction of mediaeval Britain seem a bit fastidious. And, oh yes, sticky carpets.

Well actually it wasn't nearly as bad as that and we didn't have to interact much with the fridge or the worktops. But we did have to use the shower and it wasn't a pretty sight. Actually, they had a boy's shower and a girl's shower, and I would love to comment on gender differences in student cleanliness but didn't want to risk the misunderstanding this might cause. So I can only report on the boys. Not good. Not actually blocked with body hair and the residue of several gallons of Herbal Essences but not far off it. The only bit you could actually call clean was the button you pressed to make it come on by virtue of it being poked at least three times a day in a way roughly equivalent to a wiping motion. Over the rest we draw a veil. And therein lies the dilemma. I can well remember staying in a flat myself a mere thirty or so years ago when the Mum of one flatmate came to visit. How we laughed at the thirty seconds or so it took her from crossing the threshold to attacking the cooker with a tube of Vim and a Brillo pad. None of us thought it was needed or even particularly an improvement but it seemed to make her feel happy and useful so where's the harm? Now the cream cleanser is on the other foot. Believe me, I've doused myself in filthy showers with the best of them (so to speak), but it has to be said, not for some time. And by now I seem to have lost the knack. It was on the point of making me want to scratch on the way out.

So what should parents do when confronted with almost grown up kids living in squalor? In other words, to clean or not to clean. Let's face it, they don't care and (as in my own case) may find any efforts on their behalf a subject of mild amusement. We (on the other hand), find the whole thing distinctly uncomfortable and want to do something to restore normal standards of human decency. And while trying to kid ourselves we're doing it for them, we know we're really doing it for ourselves. An odd sort of "this is hurting me more than it's hurting you y'know."

In connection with this I recently learned a new phrase of modern psychobabble that seems to cover it. Folk our age with kids in the millennial generation are apparently "helicopter parents" intent on hovering around making sure things are ok long after our parents had got rid of us and taken up an allotment or caravanning. It seems we just can't leave them alone to get on with it and clean their own cooker. Or not as the case may be.

But, if it's really for their benefit, what is actually the best thing to do? In a way it's not too different from brushing their teeth or teaching them do it themselves - it's got to be way better to build the skills than simply making sure the job gets done. But when they're toddlers you can make it happen one way or another. With kids in their 20s you can't. And I suppose that's what makes it a dilemma at all. None of us would dream of going into a friend's house and without so much as a by your leave wiping the worktops or cleaning the fridge. But for our kids - even our 20 something kids - there is still a remarkably strong drive to help. We still want to make it right, whatever that might mean. Which is a strange sensation. To begin with we're delighted at the next age appropriate step towards independence but then reality sets in. Part of the deal is that they should get to choose how dirty the shower and the carpets are. Full stop.

So, I guess you're wondering who broke first. Did we run for cover and shower at the Swimming Pool or give in and attack the white plastic with industrial disinfectant and a fire hose. Well, sad to say we hovered right down to shower level and did the deed. That's to say one of us other than me did. So everyone enjoyed a couple of days of whiter than whiteness before things started getting sticky again. Was that the right thing to do? I'll leave you to decide but I for one enjoyed the final result. And you'll be proud to know I resisted the temptation to wash a single cup. For his own good you know.